INSTINCT Workbook

The Power
to Unleash
Your Inborn Drive

T. D. JAKES

UMI (Urban Ministries, Inc.)
Chicago, IL

Copyright © 2014 by UMI (Urban Ministries, Inc.)
www. urbanministries.com
All rights reserved.
Published in the United States by UMI (Urban Ministries, Inc.),
P. O. Box 436987, Chicago, IL 60643-6987

ISBN 978-1-45555-403-4

Library of Congress Cataloguing-in-Publication Data

Jakes, T. D.
    Instinct Workbook / T. D. Jakes
    128 p. 21.272 x 27.622 cm.
    Includes Appendix
    ISBN: 978-1-45555-403-4
1. Christian Living/Inspirational. 2. Educational Supplement

Printed in the United States of America

Design of Cover by: Bruce Donaldson
Design of Book by: Bruce Donaldson
Proofreading by: Ben Sartore

10 9 8 7 6 5 4 3 2 1

First Edition

Table of Contents

INSTINCT Workbook
How to Use This Workbook

The INSTINCT Workbook is a companion to INSTINCT, by T. D. Jakes. How you use this workbook will depend on the purpose you have in mind. Did you select this workbook because you want to lead or participate in a small group experience centered on reading INSTINCT? Are you looking for new strategies that will energize and enrich your understanding of an instinctive life? Have you been searching for ideas that will empower your journey as you seek to combine your spiritual growth, intellectual potential, and the wellspring of wisdom within you? If you answered "yes" to any of these questions, then you've selected the right workbook.

Each of the 21 chapters in the INSTINCT Workbook is perfect for a small group/book club, a workshop series at a retreat, or time which you set aside regularly for focusing on your personal development. Whether you've participated in a book club or leadership retreat before, or are just looking for new ways to appreciate your untapped wisdom, these strategies and questions will provide insight to engage you as a lifelong learner. These helpful approaches will provide meaningful, thought-provoking opportunities for interactivity—with friends, family members, co-workers, people at church—even as you begin to look inside yourself and notice how you can increase your ability to move forward as your own best resource for experiencing an instinctive life. We are caretakers of God's creative genius—the time is now for refining how we show that we know this!

The format of each chapter in the INSTINCT Workbook is simple and user-friendly. "Before you begin…" and a closing remark introduce and culminate the topic in discussion, all of which align with the chapters in INSTINCT:

- INSTINCT BASICS gives you a chance to pause and consider, in an interactive way, how the chapter's topic relates to where you are and how you are presently.
- MORE ABOUT INSTINCTS offers you a chance to check in with how you're proceeding in your increasing knowledge of the topic under way.
- INSTINCTIVE WISDOM reinforces your understanding of a topic by pointing you toward relevant content from INSTINCT that can build upon the messages emerging within you.
- INSTINCTS IN ACTION is like a springboard—a platform of ideas, questions, and resources, from which you can extend your developing awareness and translate your growth into action.

In addition, because life is multi-faceted, you'll find a questionnaire in the Appendix, an "Instinctive Animal Evaluation" that's just for fun, to help you discover which animal you most resemble in your instinctive inclinations.

Enjoy your time with this INSTINCT Workbook as you hone your instincts and discover the power of your true self!

~A Letter from T. D. Jakes~
Unleash Your Instincts!

Dear Friend,

I have never been more excited about a big idea than I am about following your instincts! While on safari in South Africa, I encountered a life-transforming moment as I sat between our two guides—one an expert Ph.D. in zoology and the other a native Zulu tribesman. The zoologist told me everything I could ever want to know about the many wild animals we encountered that day. However, the Zulu knew where to find them!

After a lifetime honing his instincts, the old Zulu took in all the data he so meticulously observed, from the scent on the wind to the width of broken branches near our trail, and processed it through his internal experience. There was no doubt he clearly trusted his instincts. While the zoologist was well educated about each animal's habits, the native tribesman received his education firsthand.

As I share in my book INSTINCT, my concern is that in our twenty-first century technologically advanced culture we move farther and farther away from trusting our natural inborn drive for success. We pursue diplomas and degrees, investigate internships and infrastructures, learn new software systems and social media skills, but we rarely get in touch with the God-given wisdom already residing within us.

From my experience and observations, our true identity rarely enjoys the freedom to emerge without first enduring conformity, social modification, or outright suppression. Peer pressure, our family's expectations, and the demands of our circumstances all exert various amounts of force on who we really are. Our instincts may have even guided us to hide parts of ourselves in order to keep them alive when we were younger. We instinctively knew that we could not express our creativity, unleash our imagination, or announce our dreams without them being injured by the ridicule, rejection, or retaliation of others.

Now, however, we have the power to liberate ourselves. We need no one else's permission to unleash the God-given essence of our identity! Whether you think you have the time, money, or other resources needed to uncover who you really are, it's vitally important that you discover your core and allow it to grow, develop, and flourish. This journey of self-discovery won't be easy, but if you have the courage to look within yourself and embrace all that you find there, your instincts can become a treasure map to your soul's satisfaction.

The clues are all around you if you're willing to look and listen. Your instincts can guide you to what you love but may not have allowed yourself to admit. They can help you recall the favorite memories of childhood and what gave you pleasure then. Was it building new, never-before-seen structures with Legos? Creating stories about your friends set on another planet? Caring for your pets with the love and attention of a new parent? Composing music on your phone app? Whatever once had the power to float your boat can still rock your world!

Nothing is off-limits as you explore the jungle of your own jurisdiction. You are the most fascinating person you will ever know! So don't cover up, deny, suppress, or pretend otherwise. Allow the true you to come out, the softer side, the edgier side, the creative side, the more organized side, the driven side, the liberated side, the "who cares what people think" side, and the "this makes me feel alive" side.

This is the soil where you will discover seeds planted long ago waiting to burst through the surface of your consciousness and bear fruit. This is the galaxy of stars that can illuminate your journey through whatever darkness you may encounter. This is the area that can give you the satisfaction of knowing that you and you alone are doing what only you can do.

If this excavation process intrigues you, then I invite you to spend some time uncovering your greatest vital resources. I've created this workbook to assist you in this process. Used as a companion to enhance and complement your reading of INSTINCT, this guide will enable you to access your instincts, to discern how to use them, and to practice applying them in all areas of your life.

We'll explore how you can become more self-aware of your instinctive gifts and when to supplement this awareness with information and education. Within these pages you will find exercises, tools, homework, and suggestions to ignite the tinder of talent already inside you. While these supplements are no substitute for the lifelong learning process, they can help you discern and utilize your greatest resource: your own instincts.

If you've wondered what you're missing, then now is the time to realize the answer—nothing! You already have all you need. It's simply a matter of going within and becoming acquainted with a vital part that's waiting to be exercised more fully. Once you grasp what's already within reach, then you can move mountains! Throughout this process, I will be here to coach, counsel, and cheer you on. Follow your instincts and you will discover the wild and wondrous territory—your most successful, dynamic future—blazing ahead!

Instinctively excited and grateful for all you're about to discover,

T. D. Jakes

Instinct
Has a Rhythm

Before you begin: Please familiarize yourself with **Chapter 1** *of* INSTINCT, *pp. 1-10.*

Have you ever noticed the way the right insight at the right time can make a profound difference? In the church we often say, "God is never late, He's never early, but He's always on time!" As you begin the process of uncovering your instincts and accessing their immense wisdom and power, I suspect that the time is right. It's no accident that you're reading INSTINCT at this time and wanting to go deeper into its actualization in your own life. Something has been bubbling up within you for some time now. Call it dissatisfaction, an urge to explore, a restlessness with the status quo.

Maybe you've read other books, attended seminars, enrolled in courses, and explored other options. Regardless of the insight these other items may have afforded, you remain at the edge of a breakthrough, eager to move from the margin to the main stage of your life. I'm convinced that your instincts already know what you need to do in order to make that move.

Yes, honing your instincts requires hard work and dedication, but your personal satisfaction will ignite your desires to achieve even greater dreams. We often expend time and energy in areas of advancement outside ourselves without ever investing in what's inside us. God created men and women in His image and instilled His own divine impulse for creativity within each one. This internal compass, our instincts, can guide you beyond the trappings of success to the real treasure—the satisfaction of being and doing what you and you alone were created to be and to do.

INSTINCT BASICS

Before we jump in, let's pause and consider where you are on your journey presently and how in touch you are with your instincts. Answer each question below as honestly as possible. Don't think through your response before composing it—no one is grading you! Just begin writing as quickly and honestly as possible.

1. What brings you the greatest satisfaction in your life right now? The least?

_____

_____

_____

2. On a scale of 1 to 10, with 1 being very far away and 10 being very near, how close do you feel to living your best life, the life you know you were created to live?

1   2   3   4   5   6   7   8   9   10

Very Far Away • *Very Near*

3. Historically, what's been the greatest obstacle to moving closer to your best life? What's the largest barrier in your life right now?

_____

_____

_____

4. On a daily basis, how often do you make a decision based on your instincts?

    Never to Rarely   Once a Day   2-3 Times a Day

       4-6 Times a Day   7+ Times a Day

5. How would you define an instinct based on your understanding before reading about it in this first chapter?

_____

_____

_____

Feel the Rhythm

As I describe in this first chapter, if you don't want to take my word for it, then you only have to look to cell biology to appreciate the vital importance of our inherent instincts. At the time of conception, when the sperm and egg unite and begin forming new life, each cell has an identity with an intrinsic rhythm. Cardio-cells that will grow and unite with other cardio-cells to form a heart are already beating! Aware of their purpose, they naturally become activated to its pace. And they automatically become attracted to others beating to the same rhythm.

If our very cells are imbued with instinctive wisdom from our Creator, then how much greater is the instinctive power He's instilled in us! The building blocks of our being function as a microcosm of what we're capable of achieving if we allow ourselves to live instinctively.

When we allow our inner wisdom to filter, connect, and compare our education and our experience, our information and our insight, then we will discover the music of our life's symphony. And we will also discover others with whom we share this same tempo—people who can share our dreams and can stimulate, collaborate, and cooperate toward their fulfillment.

MORE ABOUT INSTINCTS

Before we go further, let's pause again and this time let's check in with how you're proceeding in your understanding of this chapter's topic. As you did before, answer each question below as honestly as possible. Don't think through your response before composing it—no one is grading you! Just begin writing as quickly and honestly as possible.

1. How would you describe the external rhythm of your life presently? Is it more like a slow waltz or a quick-step salsa? How does this tempo compare to the natural rhythm within you? What steps can you take to adjust the two into harmonious alignment?

   _____

   _____

   _____

2. Describe your natural instinctive rhythm as precisely as possible. What does it sound like? Is it slower and more evenly paced? Or upbeat and unpredictable? What kind of music comes to mind that reflects your natural rhythm? Is your instinctive beat more classical or country? More power ballad or pop? More techno-funk or acoustic?

   _____

   _____

   _____

3. Think about the people closest to you, friends and family of course, but also co-workers and colleagues, the people you see daily. How many of these people seem to dance to your same rhythm? Who are the people currently in your life playing at the same beat?

   _____

   _____

   _____

INSTINCTIVE WISDOM

"One of the great tragedies of life is not discovering the people culture and careers that are part of your tribe and move to the same beat. Contentment comes when you find the people, places, and events in life you were created to impact. Most individuals who lead rich, productive lives do so because they allow their instincts to guide them to the intersection of their head and heart, the place where their deepest passions and sharpest skills align with destiny. They succeed instinctively because they know their own tempo and recognize it in the individuals and institutions with whom they collaborate." —INSTINCT, pp. 5-6

Instincts may at first appear to be random emotional occurrences that come without thinking. Yet they are informed, though often even fleetingly, by our views of God, history, deeply held values, aspirations for the future, and our concern or lack of concern for people around us.

For that reason we explore these biblical characters whose instincts can provide lessons for us.

Daniel 1:1-20

CONSIDER DANIEL and his three friends. Here are four young men who arrived in Babylon from Judah—Daniel, Hananiah, Mishael, and Azariah. They had to decide in this new and strange land, whether they would abide by their religious traditions or give in to the demands of their captors. They made instinctive decisions from several perspectives.

1. What might they have considered regarding their God?

_____

_____

_____

2. What might they have recalled regarding their history?

_____

_____

_____

3. What might they have considered regarding their own future?

_____

_____

_____

4. What might they have considered regarding their people?

_____

_____

_____

5. What might they have considered regarding their knowledge of God's revealed purpose for them?

_____

_____

_____

6. What lessons can we learn about instinct as we consider the decisions Daniel and his three friends made?

_____

_____

_____

Connect to Your Calling

If we haven't discovered our instinctive rhythm, or we lose our connection to the natural tempo it provides for our life, then we often feel a sense of unease, an awareness that something's off-kilter or out of sorts. We may struggle in our relationships, stall in our career advancement, or sputter in our personal development. We watch others hit their stride and accomplish amazing feats, but we become frustrated in our efforts to imitate them. We feel stuck, unable to find a way forward to the life we can glimpse and uninterested in repeating the past.

Your instincts provide the key to your freedom. It may take several efforts to get the key to fit and the locks to turn, but I'm convinced you already know what you need to do in order to be liberated. God has given you a greater purpose than just surviving day to day, frustrated at your inability to fit in your current life. Like a poorly fitting garment, your present reality cannot contain who you were meant to be. It's time to design something bigger and better, something that fits who you are and all that you were created to do in this life. As Jesus teaches us, we should not put new wine in old wineskins (Matthew 9:14-17).

As simplistic as it may sound, if you want your life to be different, then something has to change. You're already changing and will continue to change as you proceed throughout your life. However, if you want to excel at everything you endeavor and enjoy the soul satisfaction that comes from your fulfilled purpose, then you must listen to your instincts.

INSTINCTS IN ACTION

1. When have you felt the most contentment in your life? What variables contributed to this season of satisfaction? How does this time compare to where you are now?

2. Look through family photos of yourself as a child, paying close attention to casual and candid shots of you playing, performing, and participating in various activities. What instinctive clues about your true identity stand out? What childhood pursuits still resonate with you today? What longing do they stir or what dream do they rekindle?

3. Choose one activity, hobby, or interest from childhood and begin doing a little research. While you can search for information online, you might enjoy looking at children's books on this topic. They often cover basic information in ways that capture a reader's attention and inspire her imagination.

4. Purchase a blank book, sketch pad, or new journal to use as your "Instinct Guidebook." Choose one that appeals to your senses with its shape, size, color, and texture. Decorate

it and personalize it any way you wish, as long as it clearly reflects your personality, style, and sensibilities.

5. Make your first entry in your Instinct Guidebook, journaling about your thoughts and feelings in response to what you're reading. Include the childhood item of interest from above, perhaps drawing it, pasting a picture from a magazine, or taping an online graphic you printed.

"If we seek meaning in our motives, perhaps the answer will not be the voice of God shouting at us from the heavens but in the whisper of our God-given instincts deep within" (INSTINCT, p. 8).

NOTES

_____
_____
_____
_____
_____
_____
_____
_____
_____
_____
_____
_____
_____
_____
_____
_____
_____

Basic Instincts

Before you begin: Please familiarize yourself with *Chapter 2* of INSTINCT, pp. 11-15.

Instincts are usually defined as any tendency that's genetically hardwired into a living creature, something that doesn't have to be taught or imitated. A mother bird not only knows to build nests for her eggs, but where to build them—out of sight and out of reach of predators. Many animals travel in herds while others are solo hunters. Most protect their offspring until their babies are old enough to take care of themselves, both in terms of finding food and protecting themselves. Instincts for survival motivate virtually all creatures to do whatever it takes to live, thrive, and procreate their species.

You and I are wired the same way. Babies may need to be guided to their mother's breast, but they do not have to be taught how to suckle with their mouths. It's just as natural as the production of milk in their mama's body—she didn't have to take a class to learn how to produce it! The human body seeks nourishment, protection, and comfort. "Fight or flight" remains a natural instinct that continues to guide us as we step back from the incoming car or hit someone who's hurting us.

God designed us to be resilient creatures in body, mind, and soul even as if He elevated us above all the animals. Created in His image, we bear the imprint of His divinity, including a spiritual self that is eternal. As a result, we long for more than just food, water, shelter, and protection from danger. We long for meaning in our lives, for a sense of fulfillment, purpose, and contentment. We believe we're here on this earth for a reason and remain restless until we discover it and live it. Just as our instincts can help us survive when physical needs go unmet, they can also help us fulfill our spiritual desire for meaning and joy.

INSTINCT BASICS

1. When was the last time you observed an animal or insect following its natural instincts? What intrigues you the most about what you witnessed? Do you have a similar instinct in you?

_____

_____

_____

2. How sharply attuned are you to your physical instincts? When was the last time your physical instincts prompted you to take action? Try to distinguish it from conditioning—such as eating at mealtimes.

_____

_____

_____

3. How have you experienced your spiritual longings for a meaningful life so far? In what ways have you tried to fulfill this longing? What were the results?

_____

_____

_____

Our Instincts Evolve

Our instincts serve us well as infants and children, but as we develop our instincts become more sophisticated as well. They take in more information and data and also have more personal experiences to use as a basis of comparison. However, we also become conditioned to rely on our instincts less frequently as we rely on intellect, logic, empirical evidence, science, and technology.

Assaulted by a barrage of information and sensory stimulation each day, we're prone to lose touch with the voice inside, the compelling wisdom that we often call a "gut decision" or "hunch." Others may discourage us from utilizing our instincts, insisting that they're too subjective, unsupported, or unscientific. "Stick to the facts" we're told, all the while becoming less sensitive to the natural wisdom within.

Other times we may listen to our instincts without acknowledging them as the source of a decision. We choose to go with a gut feeling about taking one job over another. We're drawn to one career field and a certain specialty rather than all the others. Certain people attract us with their ideas, charisma, and ability to inspire us. We can't always explain our choices, but we go with what seems natural.

While many times our instincts prove accurate, there are certainly exceptions. We can't simply trust our subjective opinions on every decision. We need boundaries, reality checks, and objective data that put things in perspective. We all have blind sides and need help seeing what we can't see. Over the course of our lives, we usually learn that listening to our instincts requires discernment. We have to balance external intel with internal info, allowing our instincts to synchronize and synthesize new associations, solutions, and relationships.

MORE ABOUT INSTINCTS

1. When was the last time you allowed a gut instinct or hunch to guide your final decision? What were the circumstances? Did you feel like you were taking a big risk? Why or why not?

_____

_____

_____

2. When was the last time you wished you'd listened to your instincts regarding a major decision? What were the consequences of not listening to your inner wisdom?

_____

_____

_____

3. Think about a time when your instincts were not accurate. How aware were you of their reliability at the time? Afterwards, did you remain in touch with your instincts or distance yourself because of this inaccuracy?

_____

_____

_____

INSTINCTIVE WISDOM

"Not one of us is born without instincts. A person is more likely to be born without sight than to be born without insight. In fact, many of my blind friends rely upon insight even when they have no optical illumination with which to see as we do. All of us have internal senses beyond the physical with which we can better determine what's next, what's safe, or even what's right. Our instincts speak to us daily, prompting us to pay attention, to listen more carefully, to sidestep danger and to seize an opportunity." —INSTINCT, p. 13

Instincts may at first appear to be random emotional occurrences that come without thinking. Yet they are informed, though often even fleetingly, by our views of God, history, deeply held values, aspirations for the future, and our concern or lack of concern for people around us.

For that reason we explore these biblical characters whose instincts can provide lessons for us.

Genesis 42:1-4

CONSIDER JACOB. He instinctively refused to let Benjamin go to Egypt with his brothers. Joseph's brothers had sold him to the Midianites who, in turn, sold him to Potiphar. After a stint with Potiphar, he ends up in prison; from there, he rises to become the Prime Minister of Egypt. When a famine emerges in Jacob's country, he considers sending his sons to Egypt to buy food to sustain their families. But he is reluctant to let Benjamin go with them. His instincts kick in as he ponders this decision.

1. What might Jacob have considered regarding God?

_____

_____

_____

2. What did Jacob consider regarding Joseph's experience? What other historical considerations might he have thought about in making this decision?

_____

_____

_____

3. What might he have considered regarding his and his family's future?

_____

_____

_____

4. What might he have considered regarding his knowledge of God's revealed purpose for him?

_____

_____

_____

5. What lessons can we learn about instinct as we consider Jacob's decision to prevent Benjamin from going with his brothers to Egypt?

_____

_____

_____

You Just Know

Whether it's a sense that a new project is not what it appears or your impression that a new employee is a great investment, our instincts provide us with filtered information. We may or may not be aware of the experiences, observations, and incidents that go into our instinctive filter, but they are there. And often you may not be able to articulate how you know, but your confidence remains unshaken. Some things you just know!

And regardless of whether you realize it consciously or not, you know more about yourself than you realize. Because taken together, all the data you need—both objective and subjective—

about who you are, what your unique talents are, and how to achieve their fulfillment is already in place. Whether you're young or old, married or divorced, employed or unemployed, you have distilled the essence of what you've learned about yourself and your life into your instincts.

Like a fine perfume, this instinctive essence can surprise you, inform you, and protect you if you'll let it. God wastes nothing, including our worst disappointments, most embarrassing failures, and costliest mistakes. Each event, experience, and encounter in our lives provides one more variable that ultimately strengthens our innate knowledge.

The challenge, of course, is unpacking this stored wisdom and accessing it deliberately as needed. A good place to start is identifying what you already know that you know: your preferences, your pet peeves, your personal likes and dislikes. This instinctive collection of distilled wisdom can then establish a foundation to which you return. It can steer you in directions to research what you don't know and fill in the gaps in your own instinctive knowledge. So with this in mind, let's think about what you know—and better yet, start acting on it today!

INSTINCTS IN ACTION

1. In one sentence each, write down the three most important instinctive truths you've learned about life so far. Be as specific as possible to your own life, not just, "Life is hard," but something like "I've learned life can be hard because of _____; however, I've also realized _____."

   First Truth: _____
   _____
   _____

   Second Truth: _____
   _____
   _____

   Third Truth: _____
   _____
   _____

2. Now, what specific experiences, events, people, information, and observations have led you to each of these Three Truths? Think through each one and jot down all the variables that come to mind. For instance, let's say your First Truth might be, "I've learned that in order to achieve your dreams you need support from people who believe in you." Considering what's shaped this distilled truth, you might jot down things like "starting my own business, trying to go it alone right after I graduated, my best friend showing up for that awards ceremony, that time I spoke with our CEO."

Variables contributing to First Truth: _____

_____

_____

Variables contributing to Second Truth: _____

_____

_____

Variables contributing to Third Truth: _____

_____

_____

3. Finally, what have you learned about yourself in light of these Three Truths? How has each of these influenced a recent decision you've made? Have these Three Truths affected your life in more positive ways or more negative ways? How so?

_____

_____

_____

4. Write a summary paragraph in your Instinct Guidebook about what you know you know, including your Three Truths. Illustrate each of these three instinctive distillations of wisdom with an appropriate symbol—a star, a compass, a tree, a mountain, or whatever occurs to you.

_____

_____

_____

"God, the master designer, has equipped us with a fundamental instinct that draws us to our divine purpose" (INSTINCT, p. 14).

NOTES

_____

_____

_____

_____

Instincts in Action

Before you begin: Please familiarize yourself with *Chapter 3* of INSTINCT, pp. 16-28.

As I share in Chapter 3 of INSTINCT, I often learn by what I've observed. This is intrinsic to my nature. Even as a boy, I enjoyed watching nature as well as other people in their natural habitats. I was especially drawn to people who seemed confident, content, and contagious with their sense of joyful purpose. These people continue to intrigue me to this day, and I've been privileged to observe, discuss, and interact with some of the world's most fascinating leaders, actors, musicians, scientists, athletes, and scholars.

While they each perform with excellence in different arenas, they share a common denominator: they continuously hone their instincts and put them into action. These successful individuals have not relied on others to define their roles or to determine their destinies. They have not followed anyone else's script but their own. They are not afraid to improvise, innovate, and insert themselves into risky situations that require creative solutions. They welcome change and view it as essential to their instinctively successful evolution.

INSTINCT BASICS

1. What message did you receive while growing up about what it took to be successful? What message did you receive about what it meant to follow your instincts? Did the two messages intersect in any way during your childhood and adolescence?

_____

_____

_____

2. Who are the people you grew up admiring, both locally as well as on a national or international level? What specifically did you admire about them? To what did you attribute their success?

_____

_____

_____

3. When have you tried to imitate the success of someone you admired? What were the results? What did you learn about yourself from this attempt? In what way did it sharpen your instincts for your own success?

_____

_____

_____

Highly Evolved

In many ways, our parents and families of origin shape our views on what it takes to be successful. Mine certainly did, even as they pushed beyond the roles and responsibilities assigned to them by society and stretched toward visions of success for future generations. My parents wanted me and my siblings to know that there were worlds beyond the small community in West Virginia where we grew up. They exposed us to art, intellect, and culture in order to whet our appetite for more.

When you follow your instincts, they will guide you toward more of what you long to know and experience. And then they will take you beyond it all! Whether presidents or performers, movie stars or sports stars, most highly successful people have an insatiable curiosity about life—other people, other cultures, other ideas, other ways of doing things. They look for connections that others miss and use them to build bridges to their own dynamic futures. They aren't afraid to take risks, knowing they will gain information and insight even if they fail the first few times.

MORE ABOUT INSTINCTS

1. What did your parents teach you about what it means to be successful? How were their expectations and guidance shaped by their generation, location, and society? What was distinct about their view of success when compared to these other factors?

_____

_____

_____

2. What play, field trip, concert, or cultural event ignited your imagination when you were growing up? Did a particular performer stir something in your soul? A work of art beckon you to another world? A trip away from home open your eyes to a bigger world?

_____

_____

_____

3. What's the most recent person, event, or opportunity that has ignited your imagination? What did this encounter rekindle inside you? How did you instinctively react to what it stirred up?

_____

_____

_____

INSTINCTIVE WISDOM

"Trailblazing people move by instinct because there is nothing outward that suggests that what they see inwardly is possible. Like a good detective on a crime scene, they look for clues but don't ignore the unsubstantiated hunches that have often solved cases. They combine instincts with intellect to discover a new way of seeing what's missing in plain sight."—INSTINCT, p. 21

Instincts may at first appear to be random emotional occurrences that come without thinking. Yet they are informed, though often even fleetingly, by our views of God, history, deeply held values, aspirations for the future, and our concern or lack of concern for people around us.

For that reason we explore these biblical characters whose instincts can provide lessons for us.

Joshua 2:1-22

CONSIDER RAHAB'S INSTINCTIVE BEHAVIOR. The Israelite spies arrived in Jericho to look around secretly in preparation for entering the Promised Land. Word reached the king of Jericho that spies were at Rahab's inn. She had to decide what to do. Rather than turn the Israelite spies over to the officials, she decided to protect them by hiding them on her roof underneath stalks of grain. Consider what might have entered Rahab's mind as she pondered her decision.

1. What might Rahab have considered regarding her idol gods? What might she have considered about Israel's God?

_____

_____

_____

2. What historical considerations might she have thought about in making this decision?

_____

_____

_____

3. What did she instinctively consider regarding her family's future? (See vv. 12-13.)

_____

_____

_____

4. Even though her knowledge of Israel's God was limited, what might she have considered regarding God's purpose for Israel and her people?

_____

_____

_____

5. What lessons might we learn about instinct as we consider Rahab's decision to protect the Israelite spies?

_____

_____

_____

Extra Edge

Instinctively successful people are inspired by what they experience, but also by what they lack. They know that using the resources at hand to create something new, fresh, different, and innovative often produces greater results than relying on old ways or lamenting what you don't have. When your instincts lead you, they can elevate the mundane into the magical, transforming common ingredients into uncommon results.

As kids, most of us practiced the art of using our imaginations on a regular basis. The sandbox became the Sahara and the family dog became a camel as we transformed our surroundings through our creative vision. We didn't have to have actual props and visuals to create a scene, let alone a computer—we imagined it into being!

This imaginative muscle is the same one that gets exercised any time we face a problem for which we don't have an immediate solution. When old solutions no longer suffice, we must create new ones. We have to see beyond the literal as well as through the negative and envision a passage to the other side. When our options are limited and our resources depleted, then our instincts provide us with the extra edge we need to find a way forward.

Every adversity is the seed of an opportunity waiting to sprout. Instinctively successful people know not to take no for an answer. They push beyond the boundaries of barriers and persevere to new heights. When no other solutions present themselves, then it's time to create a new one. It's risky, it's hard work, it's demanding—and it's exhilarating!

INSTINCTS IN ACTION

1. Make a list of the ten people who continue to inspire you the most. Write their names and one sentence about why they inspire you in your Instinct Guidebook. Find a picture of each one online or elsewhere and paste it next to your entry.

2. What are the works of art, music, theater, and literature that stirred something deep within you? Brainstorm a list of these and add them to your Guidebook as well.

3. Choose one place or event that you've never visited or attended and make a date with yourself. Attend an opening at an art gallery, peruse the latest exhibit at a history museum, or take in a Broadway production. Explore the botanic gardens, the opera, the children's theater, a professional sporting event, or a pottery class. Choose whatever sparks your interest and make plans for your instinctive outing.

"Barriers can become breakthroughs; they're merely blessings camouflaged as burdens. Whether you are wrestling with a poor marriage, a pathetic career, or a plummeting business, there isn't any area of your life that will not be transformed by your instincts if you're willing to look within and exercise them. If you go beyond the facts and failures and explore the feelings and impulses you have to increase what you've been given, you will light a trailblazing torch that will illuminate your steps, spark your dreams, and nourish your aspirations."—INSTINCT, pp. 27-28

NOTES

_____

_____

_____

_____

_____

_____

_____

_____

_____

_____

_____

The Elephant
Is Ova Dere!

It was the opportunity of a lifetime. While I had been incredibly blessed to travel to dozens of countries around the world and visit indelible cultures and their peoples, I had never been on an actual safari before. But after speaking at a conference in Johannesburg, I was invited by my host to travel beyond the city and encounter wild animals, ones I had only previously witnessed at the zoo, in their natural habitat. I felt like the proverbial kid in the candy store, delighted by the rugged beauty of the untamed wilderness. Little did I know how life-changing that safari would be!

As I describe in Chapter 4 of INSTINCT, our party bounced along rutted roads and overgrown trails through the African bush. We saw zebras and giraffes, monkeys and gazelles. But the mighty elephant remained elusive. Our safari guide held a Ph.D. in zoology and educated us with dozens of facts about all the animals we had seen, as well as the one we hadn't. When we still had not spotted an elephant toward the end of the day, we finally recruited another kind of expert—a Zulu tribesman.

The contrast could not have been drawn more sharply. Our animated zoologist had memorized hundreds of facts and could access all kinds of encyclopedic information about elephants with the click of his iPad. The native tribesman, on the other hand, remained stoic and silent, taking in every detail of the jungle. Until he finally asked the driver to stop and pronounced, "The elephant is ova dere!"

INSTINCT BASICS

1. What trip away from home has had the greatest impact on you? What were its major differences from what you were used to back at home? What were its major differences from what you expected?

_____

_____

_____

2. Based on your education, job experience, and other professional training, what area or field are you most knowledgeable about? Do you consider yourself an expert? Would others?

_____

_____

_____

3. Based on your life experiences, personality, observations, and aspirations, what area or field are you most instinctively drawn to explore? Is this the same area as your educational and professional experience?

_____

_____

_____

Water for Elephants

Both guides, the zoologist and the Zulu, possessed considerable knowledge about the African jungle and its inhabitants. However, there was a crucial difference informing their respective educations. The zoologist had spent hundreds if not thousands of hours studying biology, ecology, and zoology. He had read countless books and professional papers, watched dozens of recorded footage of the bush, and traveled extensively in the bush himself.

The Zulu, however, had lived his entire life in the semi-arid environment of southern Africa. He had grown up running alongside animals that the zoologist had only seen behind the fence of a zoo before entering his profession. This native tribesman had spent years and years learning the ways of the bush. He could sniff the wind and tell which animals would be coming toward us and how long it would take them to arrive. He could predict the weather by watching the clouds, monitoring the temperature with his own innate thermometer of experience, and knowing the intricacies of the dry season and the rainy season. His education was purely hands-on.

Both men relied on their instincts in different ways, but when it came time to find an elephant, the Zulu wasted no time! His instincts were developed, honed, and refined by his direct experiences, not someone else's. He knew the knowledge that can only be cultivated through the internalization of the external world around him.

Often we learn about something but we fail to learn the heart of the thing itself. We can read all kinds of business models, company histories, mission statements, and quarterly reports—and we should in order to make informed decisions—but if we've never stepped inside the building, met its employees, or used its products, then we're lacking critical experience. Similarly, we can read dozens of great romance novels, watch lovers relate in the movies, and study the psychology of attraction. But if we never risk our hearts to care for another person, then we know little about the actuality of love.

MORE ABOUT INSTINCTS

1. When have you relied on information rather than firsthand experience to make a decision? And vice versa—when have you relied on your experience instead of the available facts about a certain situation?

_____

_____

_____

2. Name one area in which your instincts should be highly developed based on the amount of time you've invested in direct experience. Parenting? Banking? Sales? Home repairs? Writing? Teaching? Baking? Cleaning? Talking?

_____

_____

_____

3. Consider the following scenario: You've just taken a new job in a city hundreds of miles away from your present home. You will need to find a new home for you and your family as soon as possible. Which of the following three people would you most want to talk with about your impending move? List your reason for choosing each of your three below your selections.

_____ Top real estate agent in your new locale

_____ Your boss at the new job

_____ A co-worker with kids the same age as yours who moved there three years ago

_____ Pastor at a large, popular church in your new city

_____ Retired teacher who has lived her entire life in your new city

_____ Old friend from high school who now lives near your new office

_____ Construction foreman for leading homebuilder in your new city

_____ Restaurant owner in the neighborhood you like best in the new city

INSTINCTIVE WISDOM

"In order to harness your intentions with your actions, you must rely on instincts. Every visionary learns that they must be well-informed and well equipped to accomplish their targeted achievements. But they must also be in touch with their instincts in order to use their experience, education, and equipment to fulfill their expectations. Instincts can help connect the dots between where you're trying to go and how you will ever get there." —INSTINCT, p. 34

Instincts may at first appear to be random emotional occurrences that come without thinking. Yet they are informed, though often even fleetingly, by our views of God, history, deeply held values, aspirations for the future, and our concern or lack of concern for people around us.

For that reason we explore these biblical characters whose instincts can provide lessons for us.

Exodus 2:1-10

CONSIDER JOCHEBED [JOK-a-bed], THE MOTHER OF MOSES. Jochebed's actions revealed her informed instincts. She was the wife of Amram and the mother of Aaron, Moses, and Miriam. Despite the edict of Pharaoh that all male infants were to be thrown into the Nile River, Jochebed's instincts led her to act contrary to the Pharaoh's command. She placed her infant in a basket and left him in the river in the care of his sister Miriam. Pharaoh's daughter found him and fell in love with Moses. Miriam, sister of Moses, prompted by her mother Jochebed, suggested Moses' mother as a nurse for the baby. Jochebed poured into Moses knowledge of God, her people, and her values. Ultimately, Jochebad had such a profound influence on Moses that he chose "affliction with the people of God [rather] than to enjoy the passing pleasures of sin" (Hebrews 11:25, NKJV).

1. What might Jochebed have considered about God when she chose to defy Pharaoh's edict that all male infants be thrown into the Nile?

_____

_____

_____

2. What historical considerations might she have thought about in making this decision?

_____

_____

_____

3. What could she have considered regarding her family's future?

_____

_____

4. What might she have considered regarding her knowledge of God's purpose for Israel and her people?

_____

_____

_____

5. What lessons might we learn about instinct as we consider Jochebed's decision to defy Pharaoh and protect her son?

_____

_____

_____

The Guide Inside

If you want to find the "elephant" you're seeking in your own life, then you must follow your instincts and not just your intellect. You certainly want as many facts as possible about any endeavor you're about to attempt. There's never an excuse for not doing due diligence unless there's absolutely no time for it. However, even when you have all the available information spread about before you, there's still something missing.

Each of us sees the world differently. If you've ever been involved in a fender bender and talked to witnesses, then you know that each one likely saw the accident a different way. Similarly, relationships, board meetings, and classroom interactions can seem one way to one party and yet be read—or misread—entirely different by others in attendance. While this makes communication and collaboration challenging at times, it also reinforces the priceless gift contained in each person's unique perspective.

Why do people see the same event, person, or meeting differently? Because we're filtering it through what we already know, what we want to know, and what we expect to find out. Sometimes we have to pay closer attention in order to sharpen our instincts. If we're missing details because we didn't observe accurately, then we cannot expect our instincts to be on target. If we're ignoring factual information, then our instincts will not be as strong as if we have all the pieces.

The key to harnessing your instincts into action is examining the variables that go into your instinctive fuel tank. Certain experiences may bias us with no good reason except for a one-time encounter. Other preferences may not be pertinent to the decision at hand; we may love brown eyes but they should not affect our choice of doctor.

We have to take our lenses apart and consider each one separately, noting how each one colors what we take in individually as well as in conjunction with the other lenses. If want to know where to find the elephant with the same acutely keen instincts as the Zulu tribesman I encountered, then we must be willing to explore the jungle within our own hearts.

INSTINCTS IN ACTION

1. Without stopping to think about it, answer this question as quickly and honestly as you can: What is the "elephant" you're currently searching for in your life? How are you currently pursuing it? What's been your experience so far with your search?

_____

_____

_____

2. As we've seen, our instincts combine a variety of external and internal variables to create a filter for how we take in information, assess it, and reach decisions. All of the following variables contribute to most people's instincts. As you think through your specific responses, also consider which of these variables you rely on most frequently.

What are the key losses in your life that influence your instincts?

_____

_____

_____

What are the big achievements in your life that affect your instincts?

_____

_____

_____

What personal biases involving other people are likely to undermine the accuracy of your instincts? What's the basis for these biases?

_____

_____

_____

What areas of special interest currently inform your instincts?

_____

_____

_____

3. What future expectations contribute to your instincts?

_____

_____

_____

What past wounds shape the accuracy of your instincts?

_____

_____

_____

What present action can you take today to improve your instincts' reliability?

_____

_____

_____

"Living by instinct elevates your ability to know where you're going and how to get there. It can help you know when to slow down and step back and when to accelerate and step up" (IN-STINCT, p. 34).

NOTES

_____

_____

_____

_____

_____

_____

_____

_____

_____

_____

_____

_____

_____

Instinct
or Extinct

Before you begin: Please familiarize yourself with *Chapter 5* of INSTINCT, pp. 37-46.

With our instincts, as with many aspects of life, we often get what we expect to get. As I share in Chapter 5 in INSTINCT, I was reminded of this truth several years ago when I wanted to purchase some land and build affordable housing in my community. While my intentions were good, I stumbled across numerous studies and dozens of statistics raising a huge red flag: many residents of low-cost housing expect their homes to be poor in quality and treat them accordingly. These residents display what we all experience in one form or another: We often behave based on our perceptions and misperceptions rather than on the reality of our situations.

Doing further research, I discovered that mixed-income housing creates the greatest opportunity for a healthy, successful community. Mixed-income housing increases the tax base, which in turn improves schools, roads, and public services. Instead of becoming isolated and defensive, neighbors learn from one another and grow to appreciate each other's differences.

I'm convinced the same mixed-variable model applies to our instincts as well. We can't rely on our instincts exclusively and expect them to be accurate and reliable every time. Similarly, we cannot ignore them and base decisions solely on facts and figures. The solution is to balance one with the other, allowing data to inform our instincts and our instincts to read between the lines of the data. If you're going to sharpen your instincts into a viable tool for actualizing your dreams, then you must be willing to keep them tethered to objective, factual information. When the two work in tandem, you will grow by leaps and bounds!

INSTINCT BASICS

1. Do you consider yourself more of a logical, rational kind of person or more of an emotional, experiential type? More of a "left-brain" individual who likes linear, sequential information? Or more of a "right-brain" creative who assimilates information more by associative patterns?

_____

2. Think of a time in the past when you contributed to a self-fulfilling prophecy by settling for what you expected to get. How did your perceptions of the situation prevent you from seeing matters more objectively? How did your perceptions in turn impact your instincts' accuracy?

_____

3. When have you made a balanced decision based on a combination of instinct and information? What were the results? What prevents you from taking a more balanced approach with most of your decisions?

_____

_____

_____

Instinct of Identity

My twin sons continue to fascinate me. Ever since they were born, each has seemed intent on asserting his distinct personality and individuality. From the baby crib to the crib they now call home, both have explored the world around them in ways that were unique to their very different personalities. Part of their motivation may have stemmed from being a twin. As much as they enjoyed having a sibling the same age with whom to share all aspects of life, no one wants to feel like someone else's clone.

As a result, my sons set out to explore, excavate, and experiment with all that they found inside themselves. Like many of us when we were growing up, they tried different styles of clothing, music, and self-expression until they found one that seemed natural. Perhaps with this goal in mind, imitation has a place in the process of developing and honing our instincts. As long as we're merely "trying on" the garments of another person's styles, successes, and selections, we can discover what truly fits.

As grown men now, my twin sons know that their uniqueness is part of their inherent value and priceless gift back to the world. There's no attempt to try and be like one another, nor is there any reaction to prove that they are so distinct and different. I'd like to think they've achieved an awareness of the unconditional love, acceptance, and affirmation that my wife and I, along with the rest of our family, want to give them. We love them just as they are, just for being who they are. I'm convinced this desire resides in all our hearts and informs the ongoing messages our instincts whisper in our heart.

MORE ABOUT INSTINCTS

1. Imagine sitting at a table in your favorite restaurant. As the lunch crowd disperses, you look over at the table across from you and see someone who appears to be your identical twin in almost every way. What do you see as you scrutinize this person? What characteristics would you use to describe someone who's your twin?

_____

_____

_____

2. How did you try to "find yourself" during your childhood and adolescence? What sports do you play? Musical instruments? What other extracurricular activities did you explore? Which interests took root as a kind of natural fit or personal passion and which ones faded away as you learned more about yourself?

_____

_____

_____

3. How would you describe your personal style when you were a teenager? Punk? Goth? Preppy? Jock? Geek chic? Designer diva? GQ gangsta? Something all your own? What fads or trends did you experiment with? Which ones seemed like a true reflection of who you are? What evidence of your fashion experimentation remains in your present style sensibilities?

_____

_____

_____

INSTINCTIVE WISDOM

"Many of us share the same variables for success as others around us and yet fail to discover our distinct, personalized combination to unlock that success. Have you ever wondered why people with less talent than you, fewer resources, and more obstacles pass you by? Have you ever attempted to follow a formula or check off five "easy steps" to fulfillment only to become frustrated and feel like you're the exception? Too often, we imitate others and conform to popular standards but fail to tap into our most powerful, most precious resource—our own uniqueness."—INSTINCT, p. 40

Instincts may at first appear to be random emotional occurrences that come without thinking. Yet they are informed, though often even fleetingly, by our views of God, history, deeply held values, aspirations for the future, and our concern or lack of concern for people around us.

For that reason we explore these biblical characters whose instincts can provide lessons for us.

Judges 4:1-16

CONSIDER DEBORAH. God called Deborah to do what few women did at that time—be a leader/judge of her people. She accepted the role, but realized the value of a male person to lead her nation's army to defeat the Canaanites. She informed Barak that God wanted him to lead their army against their foes. Barak hesitated until Deborah assured him that she would go with him to fight. She agreed to do so, but warned Barak, "'There will be no glory for you, . . . for the LORD will sell Sisera into the hand of a woman'" (Judges 4:9, NKJV). She went and Barak was successful.

1. On what basis did Deborah ask Barak to lead his people to fight Jabin's army and the Canaanites? (Judges 4:6) What did her instinct about God cause her to believe about God's help?

_____

_____

_____

2. What historical facts could she have considered in believing Barak could be successful?

_____

_____

_____

3. What did she consider about the outcome of accompanying Barak on this important mission? (See Judges 4:9.)

_____

_____

_____

4. What might she have considered regarding God's purpose for Israel and her people?

_____

_____

_____

5. What lessons might we learn about instinct as we consider Deborah's instincts in dealing with Barak?

_____

_____

_____

Decode Your Design

What catches your eye as you scroll through your email or surf online? Which ones do you read and bookmark and which do you skip and delete? Who are the people in the public eye who intrigue and inspire you by their personality, talent, and sense of style? Whose life story resonates with your own as you aspire to greater achievements in your own life?

It's never too late to unpack more of the treasure stored within you. And asking yourself questions and paying attention to what makes your heart beat faster are two of the best ways of opening this instinctive treasure chest. I've encouraged you to reminisce about your childhood as well as to reflect on some of your teenaged excursions into identity. What about where you are now? What are the threads, the through-lines of continuity and consistency, interwoven throughout your entire life? What is their pattern, the divine design that signals something greater than what you've yet accomplished?

Sometimes we need help even as we delve deeper into our own internal wisdom. The feedback of others, the results of past endeavors, and our own comments from past events can all provide priceless revelations that stimulate our instincts. Once we recognize these patterns, preferences, and proclivities, we can begin looking for larger patterns and new associations. Never forget for one moment how fascinating you really are!

INSTINCTS IN ACTION

1. Look through past performance evaluations at work, client reports, and project assessments. Review articles you've written, research papers for classes, and journal entries if you've kept one. Use an online search engine such as Google to see what the rest of the world discovers when they type in your name. What major clues to your identity stand out to you? What surprises you the most as you consider these past pieces of evidence? Jot your responses in your Guidebook.

2. Many managers and executives often take part in "360-degree" evaluations in which numerous colleagues, co-workers, clients, and associates complete an assessment and sometimes an interview regarding the subject. It's thought that seeing oneself through the eyes of major stakeholders in your career can illuminate your strengths, weaknesses, and blind spots. Conduct your own 360-degree assessment by asking key people from each of the following areas to provide written and verbal feedback on what they know and believe about the kind of person you are.

Family Area (such as spouse, sibling, adult child, or parent)
Personal Area (such as a close friend or confidant)
Career Area (such as a co-worker, colleague, or supervisor)
Community Area (such as a pastor, volunteer coordinator, or community leader who knows you well)

3. Turn to the Appendix at the end of this workbook on page 120 and take the "Animal Instinct Evaluation Questionnaire." Although it's not scientific, you might have some fun discovering your own law of the jungle!

"If you live instinctively, these critics will never impede your progress for more than a few moments. In my own life, I've never had a hater who's doing better than me!" (INSTINCT, p. 44).

An Instinctive
Sense of Direction

Before you begin: Please familiarize yourself with **Chapter 6** of INSTINCT, pp. 59-66.

Maybe you've heard the old saying, "When times get tough, the tough get tougher!" When we go through trials, adversity, and disappointments, our instincts can help us find the strength to persevere by utilizing our remaining resources. My life has been filled with numerous obstacles and barriers, but at each turn I've refused to let them impede my progress toward something greater. As I share in Chapter 6, when I was laid off from my job shortly after starting our family as well as my ministry, I knew I could not sit by passively and wait for a job to find me.

Even though it was less than ideal, not to mention a far cry from my long-range goals, I took the only steps that I saw before me. Using the meager resources I could muster, I formed a lawn care business and made the most of the desperate situation in which I found myself. While landscaping was not my primary passion, surviving a lean time was something I was definitely passionate about!

So I did what I had to do so that my family and I could continue to move forward. I didn't know how long I would have to maintain this makeshift small business, only that it was the next stepping-stone toward a greater destiny. It wasn't logical, rational, or strategic, but it was borne of necessity and desperation—two variables that sent my instincts into overdrive! If we let them, our instincts can guide us through the worst storms and allow us to find safe passage until the next safe harbor.

INSTINCT BASICS

1. When have you faced a trial or season of adversity and been forced to come up with a survival solution? How did your instincts play a role in moving through this obstacle?

   _____

   _____

   _____

2. What prevents you from trusting your instincts when confronted with a problem, conflict, or disappointment in your life?

   _____

   _____

3. What fears or concerns about your future currently prevent you from trusting your instincts more fully?

_____

_____

_____

Driving the Jeep

One of the key resources we have when faced with adversity is our team of supporting players. As I've shared many times, I felt a keen sense of responsibility to provide for my family regardless of the sacrifice involved. Similarly, I feel a sense of loyalty with my employees and want to honor their trust in me by leading our team successfully.

But these relationships work in both directions. I cannot imagine how I would have found the support to trust my instincts and take instinctive actions throughout my life without the emotional and spiritual support of my wife and family, my pastoral team and church members, and my colleagues and business associates. You need others who believe in you and affirm your instincts, not people who constantly second-guess and plant seeds of doubt. There's a place for being questioned and challenged and held accountable for our instinctive decisions, but a bond of trust must be firmly established before it can be tested.

MORE ABOUT INSTINCTS

1. Who are the key people in your life who have consistently supported you in your instinctive endeavors? Write down their names in the categories below.

Family: _____

_____

Friends: _____

_____

Colleagues and Co-workers: _____

_____

Teachers and Mentors: _____

_____

Church Family and Spiritual Leaders: _____

_____

Others: _____

_____

2. Who are the people who have caused you to doubt yourself and to ignore your instincts? What role do they currently play in your life? How can you disconnect their influence from your present and future endeavors?

_____

_____

_____

3. Who are the people you would currently like to see become more involved with your goals and aspirations? How can they help you take instinctive action to further your dreams?

_____

_____

_____

INSTINCTIVE WISDOM

"Your instincts naturally create a way forward out of whatever you have at hand. Hardship can humble you but it cannot break you unless you let it. Your instinct for survival will see you through if you're attuned to its frequency. Instinct will find a temporary stopgap without ever taking its sights off of your larger goals. There's no greater way to hone your instincts than to overcome adversity. Successful leaders know that instincts transform adversity into opportunity."
—INSTINCT, p. 57

Instincts may at first appear to be random emotional occurrences that come without thinking. Yet they are informed, though often even fleetingly, by our views of God, history, deeply held values, aspirations for the future, and our concern or lack of concern for people around us.

For that reason we explore these biblical characters whose instincts can provide lessons for us.

1 Samuel 17:1-11, 32-51

CONSIDER DAVID MEETING GOLIATH. When the Philistines and Goliath challenged the Israelites, the Israelites, including Saul, were afraid to confront their enemy. Young David came on the scene, sized up the situation, and volunteered to fight the giant. He told King Saul that his experience in killing a lion and bear gave him the knowledge and confidence to recognize that if God delivered him from these vicious animals, God would deliver him from Goliath. Consider David's instincts in this situation.

1. How did David's view of God help him to muster the courage and passion to defeat Goliath?

_____

_____

_____

2. What historical facts could he have considered in believing he could defeat Goliath?

_____

_____

_____

3. What did David believe would be the outcome of defeating Goliath? (See 1 Samuel 17:46-47.)

_____

_____

_____

4. What might David have considered regarding God's purpose for Israel and his people?

_____

_____

_____

5. What lessons might we learn about instinct as we consider David's instinctive insights, decisions, and actions?

_____

_____

_____

Scare Me Again

While most of us do not need additional fears to fight, we do need the ongoing stimulation of a healthy challenge. Once we master an area or become familiar with our responsibilities, all too often we become complacent. We settle for satisfactory instead of true satisfaction. We allow our routines to numb our instinctive sensibilities and step back from the risks needed to break out of the rut.

If we want to excel at living instinctively, then we must constantly challenge ourselves in positive, dream-affirming, talent-stretching ways. We must surround ourselves with other positive, progressive, instinctively attuned individuals who will stimulate, inspire, and motivate us to our full potential. On the other hand, we must remove ourselves from relationships—whether personal or professional—that seek to diminish our dreams and discount our directives.

We need people in our lives who are in touch with their instincts and model instinctive living and risk-taking. Trust is essential as well as mutual respect. When we encounter these kinds of people, we're able to sharpen one another's instincts as we move forward in progressive ways that are dynamic, innovative, and exhilarating!

INSTINCTS IN ACTION

1. Make a list of the people currently in your life who see your true talents and potential and challenge you accordingly. Choose at least one to invite to lunch as a thank you for their belief, support, and encouragement.

2. Describe a time when you've experienced a "scare me again" kind of moment. What was the challenge you faced? In what ways did it terrify you? Excite you? Inspire you? What role did your instincts play in going through this experience?

3. In your Instinct Guidebook, make a list of three to five successful people in your community, individuals who clearly take risks and seem comfortable following their instincts. Choose one to ask to mentor you and then email or call this person to arrange a meeting. If he or she is unavailable as a mentor, choose another person on your life until you have an "instinctive mentor" with whom you can meet at least once a month.

"I'm convinced the only way you can develop your true gifts, your creative instincts is by embracing a vision so daunting that your heart goes running up the steps like a child, screaming with delight because you have a challenge that equals your creativity" (INSTINCT, p. 60).

NOTES

_____

_____

_____

_____

_____

_____

_____

_____

_____

Instincts Turned Inside Out

Before you begin: Please familiarize yourself with *Chapter 7* of INSTINCT, pp. 67-78.

Sometimes our most glaring mistakes become our most significant milestones. When we take a risk, create an experiment, or test a hypothesis, we often discover something unexpected, unpredictable, and unprecedented. These discoveries have led many inventors and innovators to revelations, epiphanies, and products that they would never have had if they had not failed and kept trying.

If you can suspend judging and condemning yourself for your failures, then you can engage with the lessons to be learned from them. If you can ignore the criticisms and derisive comments from others, then you can absorb an instinctive awareness of what to do differently next time. Our instincts constantly monitor all that we're doing, thinking, saying, and risking, looking for insight to guide us to new heights.

Creative individuals know that they have to give themselves permission to play, to discover, to attempt, and—yes—to fail in order to unleash their talent. Painters have to make sketches of things that never end up in their paintings. Composers must endure the disharmony of discordant notes before the right combination flows together. Writers must continually draft and revise and revise some more in order to express their ideas and stories.

If creative people gave up the first time their art didn't come together, then we would have nothing but empty museums, libraries, and concert halls! Our instincts can transform our greatest trials into our most surprising triumphs if we follow their wisdom and persevere in our attempts. Like the legendary alchemists, our instincts turn lead into gold.

INSTINCT BASICS

1. In what areas of your life have you failed repeatedly? What has emerged from your efforts and attempts? How have you handled these failures in your life? What have you learned from them that has influenced your instincts?

_____

_____

_____

2. Describe the inner voice that typically criticizes your actions and condemns your intentions. If you don't have one, then count your blessings because most of us do! Who has contributed to the formation of your inner critic? Parents? Partners? Teachers? Bosses? Others?

_____

_____

_____

3. What would you instinctively like to say in response to your inner critic? What risks would you take if you knew that no one—not even yourself—would criticize your actions?

_____

_____

_____

Instinct Adapts

When faced with seemingly insurmountable adversity and hardship, our instincts enable us to adapt in order to survive. Conditions and circumstances that we could never imagine ourselves enduring and surviving somehow become manageable when we allow our instincts to lead us moment by moment and day by day. Survivors of war, slavery, brutal crimes, and natural disasters somehow find the strength and resiliency to keep going. It's devastatingly difficult and in some cases impossible to fathom. Yet the human spirit, guided by divinely designed instincts, cannot be vanquished.

In many cases, we not only survive but we discover new dimensions of our personalities. When confronted with life-threatening dangers, we often summon reserves of strength previously undetected. With our backs against the wall, we surprise ourselves with new levels of courage and creativity.

MORE ABOUT INSTINCTS

1. When have your instincts helped you adapt to new changes? What prior expectations and assumptions did you have to release in order to accept these changes? Why?

_____

_____

_____

2. How have your instincts enabled you to survive difficult circumstances? What wisdom about yourself emerged as you endured this painful season? What new abilities, talents, and gifts did you discover within yourself?

_____

_____

3. What are the greatest challenges you've overcome in your life? How have they influenced the person you are today? How have they strengthened your instinct for survival?

_____

_____

_____

INSTINCTIVE WISDOM

"When you follow your instincts and transform your vision into reality, you will discover that accidents, mistakes, and conflicts become creative material. Rarely do you have everything you think you need in order to succeed. Living by instinct allows you to adapt to change and grow stronger. Instinct often processes, learns, and accepts change before we do. Once our emotions, intentions, and abilities catch up, we move forward, one step closer to seeing our dreams realized."—INSTINCT, p. 70

Instincts may at first appear to be random emotional occurrences that come without thinking. Yet they are informed, though often even fleetingly, by our views of God, history, deeply held values, aspirations for the future, and our concern or lack of concern for people around us.

For that reason we explore these biblical characters whose instincts can provide lessons for us.

Genesis 39:1-23; 45:1-8; 50:16-21

CONSIDER JOSEPH. Joseph's brothers ridiculed him when his father made him a coat of many colors. They hated him and sold him into slavery in Egypt, and he became a slave of Potiphar. Potiphar's wife lied on him and as a result Potiphar threw him into prison where he remained until Pharaoh's butler remembered him and recommended him to Pharaoh. Joseph underwent numerous trials and negative experiences before Pharaoh promoted him to be the Prime Minister of Egypt. How did his instincts guide him toward success?

1. What was Joseph's view of God that caused him to instinctively remain faithful to God during his many temptations and difficult days?

_____

_____

_____

2. What historical facts could Joseph have considered in standing firm in his convictions?

_____

_____

3. What purpose did Joseph instinctively believe God was accomplishing by permitting him to experience slavery and later serve as the Prime Minister of Egypt? (See Genesis 45:4-5.)

_____

_____

_____

4. What instinct drove Joseph's decision to forgive his brothers when they confessed their harsh treatment of him and asked him to forgive them? (See Genesis 50:16-21.)

_____

_____

_____

5. What lessons might we learn about instinct as we consider Joseph's instincts in dealing with his brothers, Potiphar, Potiphar's wife, the butler, and the baker?

_____

_____

_____

Instinct Inspires

While you might be tempted to think only artists and writers need inspiration, we all rely on our imaginations for ideas every day. If one route to work is blocked, we take another. If we can't convince a client to meet at our office, we go to her. If a big project goes off the tracks, we look for ways to restore its successful trajectory.

Our instincts will guide us beyond familiar paths and predictable solutions if we're willing to follow them outside the box. Too often, we settle for what's been done before, the way it's been done before. We limit ourselves without even realizing it. With our instincts as our muse, we can discover new patterns, brilliant systems, and amazing conceptual relationships that shake up the status quo.

Sometimes our most inspired solutions emerge from the unlikeliest places. We must remember that our instincts absorb inspiration from every direction, especially the ones that tend to surprise us most. Like Nike's co-founder Bill Bowerman creating a running shoe tread from glimpsing a waffle iron, we can make inspired associations that astound us with their practicality and functionality. Our instincts function as creative catalysts for our ultimate success. We only need to pay attention and take action.

INSTINCTS IN ACTION

1. When faced with a new project, product, or problem, how do you usually begin the process of tackling it? Do you have a kind of system or do you approach each new initiative differently? Do you usually work more productively by yourself or as part of a team?

   _____

   _____

   _____

2. In your Instinct Guidebook, make a list of anything that is currently inspiring you. These items may be photographs, articles, books, blogs, websites, paintings, sculpture, cars, interior designs, specific pieces of clothing, particular designers—anything that's appealing to you, stirring something inside you, and igniting ideas of your own.

3. Flip through a stack of magazines and focus only on visual images. Cut out any picture, graphic, image, scene, or artwork that evokes something in you. You don't have to love it—in fact, you may even hate it!—but it definitely triggers strong emotions.

4. Sort through the items you clipped and choose five to paste in your Instinct Guidebook. Beside each one, jot down why you find it so evocative, intriguing, or emotionally charged.

5. Visit an unusual place that you would not normally encounter but have always been curious about. It might be the local florist's shop, an animal shelter, a history museum, or a local tourist attraction.

"Our instincts inspire us to look beyond the usual and identify the unusual. If we're attuned, our instincts transfer principles from one field of study to another, mix metaphors that yield new insights, and create fresh designs from tired traditions" (INSTINCT, p. 73).

NOTES

_____

_____

_____

_____

_____

Instincts to Increase

Before you begin: Please familiarize yourself with *Chapter 8* of INSTINCT, pp. 79-89.

Perhaps it's human nature to want more than we have. Or perhaps it's simply the divine impulse compelling us to put into action God's instruction to Adam and Eve: "Be fruitful and multiply" (Genesis 1:28). But there is an important distinction to be made, one that's crucial to your ability to achieve instinctive success. You must be willing to be honest with yourself, look within your heart and motives, and identify greed. It's an ugly word and one we don't like applying to ourselves. But we must learn to distinguish the negative inclination to consume in order to fill a void in our lives and the positive instinct to create continually on a larger and larger scale.

Greed seeks to give us a false sense of happiness through material possessions and accumulated wealth. The instinct to increase, on the other hand, guides us to our most creative, productive arenas, the destination of our dreams where we can live out our instinctive purpose. When greed motivates us, there's never enough—not enough money, not enough stuff, and not enough time to enjoy any of it. When the instinct to increase motivates us, there's more than enough and it's continually multiplying!

Success breeds success. When we allow our instincts to guide us and achieve success in one area, we will soon discover that more doors will open. Our ability to navigate our ascension in one field transfers to increased opportunities in other fields. The financial and material success will likely follow, but it's secondary to the innate personal satisfaction that emerges when you're living out your instinctive and divinely appointed purpose.

INSTINCT BASICS

1. Have you experienced times when you struggled with your success? Ever felt unworthy or even guilty for enjoying your accomplishments? What contributes to this struggle?

_____

_____

_____

2. Have you ever considered yourself "greedy" or "too ambitious"? Have others made you feel like you didn't deserve the advancements you worked hard to achieve?

_____

_____

_____

3. When have you experienced the "instinct to increase"? How has success in one area of your life planted seeds for success in other areas? How can you tell the difference between greed and instinctive fruitfulness?

_____

_____

_____

Cages and Stages

One of the greatest barriers to your advancement is your current comfort zone. Even if you're dissatisfied and disappointed with your present circumstances, at least they seem familiar and predictable. Rather than having to take risks and venture out into a new jungle, we often settle for the back corner of the cage where we attempt to tell ourselves we're satisfied. Or we tell ourselves that our cage provides comfort and protection, that it's too risky out in the wilderness.

But something keeps drawing us back to the door, to our vision beyond the bars of our cage. Like the lion confined in his pen at the zoo, we instinctively long to experience greater freedom and a larger adventure than our cell permits. This yearning is universal; however, the timing, pace, and particular destination beyond our cage is unique. No one can tell us the right time to leave our cage of conformity, and no one can do it for us.

It's simply the magnetic attraction we have for something beyond where we find ourselves. We may not know exactly what it is we'll find but we know that we have to explore opportunities or live with regret the rest of our lives. But we don't have to live with regret. If we're willing to follow our instincts, we will discover an entire world beyond the confines of our current cage!

MORE ABOUT INSTINCTS

1. How would you describe your present circumstances? In what areas of your life are you presently most satisfied and comfortable? Which areas feel more unsettled and restless?

_____

_____

_____

2. What do you fear most about taking the risk to step out of your current cage? What would you risk losing? What could you potentially gain?

_____

_____

_____

3. When have you ventured out of your comfortable cage in the past? Which risks have allowed you to progress and experience a bigger world beyond where you began?

_____

_____

_____

INSTINCTIVE WISDOM

"Instinctively successful individuals almost always have had to go through a metamorphosis in order to free themselves from their cage-like habits. And more importantly, they need time and training to adapt and develop the instincts that are critical to survive in the new environment. If the lion needs that adaption space to migrate into what should be instinctive, we too have to be prepared to be mentored and tutored even when we possess the instinct to increase."—INSTINCT, p. 82

Instincts may at first appear to be random emotional occurrences that come without thinking. Yet they are informed, though often even fleetingly, by our views of God, history, deeply held values, aspirations for the future, and our concern or lack of concern for people around us.

For that reason we explore these biblical characters whose instincts can provide lessons for us.

Luke 1:26-38

CONSIDER MARY THE MOTHER OF JESUS. When the angel Gabriel told her God had chosen her to bring His Son into the world, Mary did not hesitate to respond positively. Even though she was just a young teen, unmarried, and could face the ridicule of carrying a baby without being married to its father, she risked her reputation by saying to the angel, "I am the Lord's servant. May everything you have said about me come true" (Luke 1:38, NLT).

1. What was Mary's view of God that caused her instinctively to respond positively to Gabriel's message that God had chosen her to give birth to God's Son, Jesus?

_____

_____

49

2. What historical information could Mary have considered in responding to the angel?

_____

_____

_____

3. What purpose did Mary instinctively believe God was accomplishing by choosing her to give birth to God's Son? (See Luke 1:48, 54.)

_____

_____

_____

4. What does Mary say in her Magnificat that reveals her concern for her people and how her Son would help them? (See 1:53-55.)

_____

_____

_____

5. What lessons can we learn about instinct from this consideration of Mary's thoughts and actions?

_____

_____

_____

Instinct to Jump

While caution and moderation are important virtues, they must be tempered by risk and decisiveness. When opportunity knocks, we must be prepared to answer the door rather than burying our head under the covers and pretending to sleep. Our instincts provide us with the sense of timing, selection, and action that allows us to take big leaps of faith.

Sometimes we may experience a plateau, especially after attaining what we thought we wanted. We get the corner office, have the beautiful home, delight in our healthy family, and have more than enough to pay the bills. We worked so hard to arrive at this place, and yet something's still missing. It's not quite what we thought it was after all. Or maybe it's exactly what we wanted but now our interests have shifted.

When we peel away the layers of conditioning, living for others, and conforming to societal expectations, we discover that instinctive risk is part of the thrill of successful living. No matter how successful you become, you will always long to fulfill your purpose. It's not the destination that brings you the satisfaction, it's the journey! Instinctively, we know this important truth, but the tricky part is living it out.

INSTINCTS IN ACTION

1. When have you achieved a major milestone in your life—a degree, a job, a promotion, a relational turning point—and felt disappointed that it didn't satisfy you the way you expected? How did you respond in that situation?

_____

_____

_____

2. What's the biggest risk you would take in your life right now if you knew you couldn't fail? What's at stake if you take this leap and fail? What can you gain?

_____

_____

_____

3. In your Instinct Guidebook, brainstorm and write a list of ten small risks you can take in the next week. These might include items like, "Ask Dr. Smith to lunch for advice about finishing my degree," or "Talk to my accountant about what's involved in launching my small business idea." Place a star next to five of these items and get started on at least one of them today.

"Your time is limited, so don't waste it living someone else's life. Don't be trapped by dogma—which is living with the results of other people's thinking. Don't let the noise of others' opinions drown out your own inner voice. And most important, have the courage to follow your heart and your intuition. They somehow already know what you truly want to become. Everything else is secondary."—Steve Jobs, INSTINCT, p. 84

NOTES

_____

_____

_____

_____

_____

_____

Instincts
Under Pressure

Before you begin: Please familiarize yourself with *Chapter 9* of INSTINCT, pp. 91-101.

When faced with the demands and pressures of life, we're often tempted to lay low and remain in the comfortable confines of our current cage. With the stress of family responsibilities, work obligations, and financial burdens, we don't feel like we have the time, energy, or resources needed to take risks. This may be true for some people since, as we've seen before, we each have our own unique instinctive pace.

However, we will always face challenges in our lives. There will always be family members who need our support, friends in crisis, deadlines at work, and financial obligations to be paid. We simply cannot allow ourselves to ignore our risk-taking instincts while we wait for the "right time." Life tends to spill over into all areas and require as much as we can give. But this doesn't mean that we don't step out in faith at crucial junctures by following our instincts.

The pressures and stressors we face each day may even indicate that we're overdue for a change! Sometimes it's more stressful staying in place and working to maintain status quo than facing our fears and embracing change. When we're guided by our instincts, we allow ourselves more choices than if we just sit by and wait for life to happen to us. Being proactive, planning ahead, and anticipating opportunities are the results when we use life's pressures in productive ways.

INSTINCT BASICS

1. What are the most stressful demands presently in your life? How do you usually handle stress? Where do you turn for relief, rest, and comfort?

   _____

   _____

   _____

2. Which relationships in your life currently require the most energy and attention? What dynamics would you change in these relationships if you could? What's preventing you from making these changes?

   _____

   _____

   _____

3. On the following scale, indicate how you usually respond to significant changes in your life:

1   2   3   4   5   6   7   8   9   10

resistant • • • • • • • • • • *tolerant* • • • • • • • • • • • • *eager* • • • • • • • • • • • • • *welcoming*

4. What changes frighten or intimidate you the most? Changes in relationships at home? At work or in your career? In your finances? With your health? Others?

_____

_____

_____

5. When have you unexpectedly benefited from a dramatic change in your life? How did you discover the gift in the midst of your discomfort?

_____

_____

_____

Instincts Like a Challenge

Perhaps it's just our innate desire to survive or to make our own choices in life. Or maybe we simply feel like we don't have a choice. When life crashes in on us, however, we do have choices—no matter what happens, we always have choices, even if they're very limited by circumstances. Maybe it's simply the fear of regret that motivates us to get back on our feet, take the next step, and resume our journey.

Regret can certainly be a powerful motivator, and our instincts know this. Most people, from research psychologists to 90-year old seniors, seem to agree that it's better to risk action and fail than to take no action and forever wonder "what if…?". When we choose not to risk, we must accept that we cannot know the results of what might have happened. So much of life is simply about showing up and engaging with the present moment and the opportunities that present themselves. If we don't take a leap of faith, then we must accept the unknown possibilities of what might have been.

Occasionally, we know that it's the right time to risk regardless of our circumstances. Changing careers, moving to a new location, or starting a relationship require enormous strength and courage. But if your instincts are guiding you, then you will eventually find yourself standing on the edge of a cliff with the notion to jump! Others may be there to support you, even to help catch you if you fall, but you alone are the only one who can step out of the cage and over the edge.

MORE ABOUT INSTINCTS

1. What important life decisions would you choose differently if you could make them over? Why would you change them? In other words, what do you regret about them?

_____

_____

_____

2. Which do you usually regret more: what you do that fails, or what you don't do that leaves you wondering what you missed? What do you regret most that you chose not to do in your life so far? What do you regret most that you've done?

_____

_____

_____

3. What's the biggest leap of faith you've made toward improving your life? What consequences have emerged so far? What have you learned? What do your instincts tell you is the next step?

_____

_____

_____

INSTINCTIVE WISDOM

"We're used to basing our decisions on past experiences and then suddenly our instincts pull us toward something equally tantalizing and terrifying. We cannot deny our instinctive attraction and yet we're unsettled by its unfamiliarity. Nothing in our repertoire of achievements and abilities, nor our family, our training, our education, or our experiences has prepared us, and yet we are drawn instinctively toward something that excites us, touches us, energizes us, and leaves us shaking in our boots."—INSTINCT, p. 93

Instincts may at first appear to be random emotional occurrences that come without thinking. Yet they are informed, though often even fleetingly, by our views of God, history, deeply held values, aspirations for the future, and our concern or lack of concern for people around us.

For that reason we explore these biblical characters whose instincts can provide lessons for us.

Exodus 2:11-15a

CONSIDER MOSES. Pharaoh's daughter plucked Moses from the Nile River and employed Moses' mother Jochebed to raise him—though she did not know Jochebed was his mother. When Moses grew up, aware that he was a descendant of Abraham, Isaac, and Jacob to whom God had made promises, he instinctively desired to liberate his people from the harsh treatment of the Egyptians. When Moses saw the Egyptians mistreating his people, he lashed out and killed an overseer for beating his fellow Israelite. His instinct to rescue his people was commendable, but the timing and method were not right. Moses had to flee the country until God called him at the right time and gave him the right methods.

1. What was Moses' view of God that caused him to instinctively want to liberate his people from oppression?

_____

_____

_____

2. What historical information might Moses have considered that led him to want justice for his Israelite brother?

_____

_____

_____

3. Do you think Moses at this juncture was aware of God's purpose for his people? How might this awareness play into his decision to kill the Egyptian?

_____

_____

_____

4. Moses could have ignored the plight of his people at this point because he himself was in a good position in the Egyptian hierarchy; instead, he instinctively chose to identify with his people. Why?

_____

_____

_____

5. What lessons might we learn about instinct from a consideration of Moses' instincts at this point in his life?

_____

_____

_____

Instinct to Fly

While others cannot make our choices for us, sometimes they can give us a nudge! Like the mother bird that knows it's time for her babies to leave the nest and try out their wings, sometimes our loved ones must remind us that it's time to move on. Other times, our circumstances may necessitate a sink-or-swim, fly-or-die-trying response. When you lose your job and have no prospects on the horizon, it's time to fly. When your spouse divorces you and you have to provide for your children, it's time to fly. When you finally complete your degree, it's time to fly.

We all have this instinct to soar in us, but life often beats it out of us. We become weary, scarred, wounded, and exhausted by all the demands and burdens placed upon us. We're tempted to stop risking, to stop caring, to stop trying, to stop hoping for anything more than what we've already experienced. We fear that best has already been and all that remains is a downhill slide toward desperation. But this is simply not true!

I sincerely believe that if we follow our instinctive rhythm, then it's never too late to risk improving ourselves. Oh, it's tempting to believe that beautiful, young, successful people are the only ones who fulfill their destiny, but nothing could be further from the truth. Over time, our true character reveals itself and we're forced to strip away surface layers, or our ego-driven pretense, and follow our true instincts. Maybe you already have regrets or wish you had made different choices. Fair enough, but what you've learned is priceless information about yourself, your desires, and your dreams. If you follow your instincts, it's never too late to succeed!

INSTINCTS IN ACTION

1. Surf on the web through travel sites and make a list of three places you've never been that you would love to visit someday. If you have the resources, choose one and begin planning a trip there later this year. If you currently don't have the means, then begin saving for such a trip, and in the meantime, download a free visitor's guide or purchase a travelogue about this place. Try to identify why it appeals to you.

_____

_____

_____

2. If you could change careers and do anything other than what you're presently doing, what field would you explore? What aspects of this career field appeal to you? Why? Do some sleuthing and try to find someone in your area who works in this other career area. Set up a time to interview them over coffee or at least have a phone conversation.

_____

_____

_____

3. If you could make one change in your body, what would it be? Why? Is this desired change due to what others think of you or something that comes from within? Or a combination of both? What do your instincts tell you about how to handle this aspect of yourself that you wish you could change? Accept it? Cover it up? Change what you can?

_____

_____

_____

"There are times when we must disregard the data and distance our doubts if we are ever going to achieve greater velocity toward the goals that roar within us. We must follow our instinct to fly" (INSTINCT, p. 97).

NOTES

_____

_____

_____

_____

_____

_____

_____

_____

_____

_____

_____

_____

_____

_____

Instincts
Set the Pace

Before you begin: Please familiarize yourself with **Chapter 10** of INSTINCT, pp. 103-115.

As we've discussed, sometimes your instincts compel you to run out of the cage, jump over the edge, and fly out of the nest. But as we've also explored, not all instinctive rhythms are the same. Often our gut instinct may be to wait until we have more capital to invest or until we have a partner in our entrepreneurial venture or until our health improves. Our instincts dispense wisdom about timing just as they inform us of what course of action to take.

If we're attuned to them, often our instincts will help us make a transition in gradual stages. Instead of leaving our cage and slamming the door shut behind us, we can take a few steps beyond the threshold and look around before returning. The next time, we can venture even farther until finally we are ready to remain in the freedom of the jungle and can't imagine returning to the confinement of our former cage.

Whether you think of it as a safety net, a Plan B, or an escape hatch, it's instinctively wise to plan for contingencies. Sometimes these other options are where our instincts actually want to lead us. Other times, they're simply ways to safeguard our resources and provide peace of mind during a time of transition.

INSTINCT BASICS

1. What's your natural instinctive pace when you take a risk? Do you tend to move quickly and sort through the consequences down the road? Or do you like to take your time and make slow, careful movements for each step along the way?

   _____

   _____

   _____

2. How do you interact with people whose instinctive rhythm is noticeably different than yours? Which type of person frustrates you more, the slow poke who causes delays and bottlenecks? Or the speed freak who's always racing ahead and impatiently waiting on others to catch up?

   _____

   _____

3. How would you describe your current pace of life? Too fast? Too slow? Just right? What's required for you to attain more work-life balance right now?

_____

_____

_____

No Turning Back

During different seasons and circumstances of life, our instinctive rhythm changes. What may have started as a fast-paced, adrenaline-fueled leap of faith may settle into a slower, more even-keeled transition. You may make the decision to switch careers and accept a new job overnight, but then you must settle into handling the details of relocating, moving, and settling into your new position.

Some opportunities may carry an automatic deadline or be available only for a limited time. When forced to make a rather quick decision, we would do well to heed our instincts' call to wisdom as well as instructive pace. We often impose a sense of urgency where none exists. We assume we must respond immediately when we could receive more time if we simply asked for it. Knowing your own needs and keeping your true best interests front and center are instinctive priorities.

Most often the choices we make and the pace we set require a commitment. We can't undo them and go back to the way things used to be in our cage. This inability to retreat may even be a blessing in disguise at times. When confronted with initial resistance or early obstacles, we might tuck tail and run back to our doghouse instead of remaining on our own in the wild. While regrets may linger occasionally, our instincts have a keen sense of moving forward. We may try to replicate the past or repeat the same patterns of behavior, but our instincts naturally take us to new heights.

MORE ABOUT INSTINCTS

1. Have you ever experienced "buyer's remorse" about a decision and wish you could undo it? How did you handle the consequences? How has the decision impacted other choices you've made?

_____

_____

_____

2. What patterns of behavior do you tend to repeat in life? Do you start getting restless and try to change jobs every five years? Do you find yourself returning to certain relationships, locations, or events on a regular basis?

_____

_____

3. When have you had second thoughts about a certain action taken only to discover it was the right one over the long haul? Are you more inclined to base decisions on short-term consequences or long-term impact?

_____

_____

_____

INSTINCTIVE WISDOM

"It's perfectly normal to be terrified of making changes. And it's perfectly normal to stumble, fall, and have to get up again and again as you make your way through your new environment. However, don't rush when you don't have to! And don't burn bridges behind you—enough of them will catch fire by themselves! If you don't have to shut the door of the cage, then leave it cracked open so that you can retreat there as needed."—INSTINCT, p. 109

Instincts may at first appear to be random emotional occurrences that come without thinking. Yet they are informed, though often even fleetingly, by our views of God, history, deeply held values, aspirations for the future, and our concern or lack of concern for people around us.

For that reason we explore these biblical characters whose instincts can provide lessons for us.

Luke 15:11-24

CONSIDER THE PRODIGAL SON. The younger son made a decision to leave home with his portion of his father's inheritance. After squandering it all in riotous living, he came to himself, returned home, and his father welcomed him back. Reflect on the son feeding swine in the pig pen as you consider the following:

1. What view of God do you think the prodigal son held before he left home? Do you see any evidence that he acted with good instincts in deciding to leave home under these conditions?

_____

_____

_____

2. In the pig pen of the far country, what historical facts did he instinctively reflect on as he pondered his next move? (See v. 17.)

_____

_____

_____

3. What values might the prodigal son have realized he violated and now wanted to rectify as he made plans to return home?

_____

_____

_____

4. What did the prodigal son say he was willing to do in the future to justify his father's reception at home? (See vv. 18-19.)

_____

_____

_____

5. What lessons might we learn about instinct from a consideration of the prodigal son's good and bad instincts?

_____

_____

_____

Stumble toward Success

Many people often ask me how I've learned to do all that I enjoy doing—preaching, speaking, teaching, writing, singing, producing, investing, and making movies to name a few. While I've certainly benefited from conventional methods of education, most of my expertise has come the hard way—from trial and error! Through experimentation, mid-course corrections, the wise counsel of others with more experience, and perseverance, I've survived a crash course in most all my endeavors.

Most instinctively successful people I know have attained their education the same way. Some have dropped out of college so they can travel and explore new options. Others have switched careers in mid-life and failed dozens of times before cracking the code of their greatest success. Many have ended up in roles, careers, industries, and occupations that they never imagined a few years ago. But they've continued to stumble forward, taking advantage of each opportunity as it comes, opening each new door, getting up and going forward over and over again.

Yes, you will encounter the naysayers, critics, and pundits who had rather take shots at others' attempts than risk anything themselves. And certainly not all criticism is harmful—much of it can help you improve areas of weakness and overcome liabilities dragging you down. But the attitude and intentionality of the person providing feedback reveals so much about their motives. If they truly want to encourage, support, and challenge you to fulfill your potential, then you will sense their constructive energy. However, if jealousy, envy, or competitive comparison fuels their motives, then you must steer clear of their intended destructive power.

Always listen when others offer you advice, feedback, or instruction. Thank them for their input and then consider it, assess it, and evaluate its worth. Ultimately, however, you can only rely on your own instincts and not anyone else's. You must move to the beat of your own drummer as you advance to the next stage of your instinctive success!

INSTINCTS IN ACTION

It's time for your mid-term examination! Don't panic—if you've made it this far, you've already earned an A+ with a gold star! You simply need to review your answers in this workbook as well as the ideas, feelings, artistic expressions, and images in your Instinct Guidebook. Answer the following questions as quickly and honestly as you can. Remember, there's no way you can fail!

1. How have your ideas about your personal instincts changed since you began reading INSTINCT and exploring this Workbook?

_____

_____

_____

2. What has surprised you most in what you discovered about yourself so far? What has confirmed what you already suspected?

_____

_____

_____

3. Which of the previous ten chapters has spoken to you in the most powerful way? What ideas and feelings has it stirred inside you?

_____

_____

_____

4. What big idea or radical change is brewing inside you right now? What are your instincts leading you to explore?

_____

_____

_____

5. Throughout the course of your day, how aware are you of your instincts operating now? How has this awareness improved your life?

_____

_____

_____

"It's not how many times you have failed; it's what you've learned each time you got back on your feet" (INSTINCT, p. 112).

NOTES

_____

_____

_____

_____

_____

_____

_____

_____

_____

_____

_____

_____

_____

_____

_____

Instinctive Investments

Before you begin: Please familiarize yourself with *Chapter 11* of INSTINCT, pp. 117-131.

When we're out of sync with our instincts, we may not realize that we've been pursuing the wrong goals for our fulfillment until we achieve them. The proverb about being careful what you wish for because you might get it often applies to our misguided efforts to find satisfaction in the souvenirs of success without having made the actual journey. Instinctive success savors the daily ups and downs, the failures and triumphs, the decisions and diversions more than any corner office, trophy, or diploma on the wall.

If you've opened the channel to greater instinctive awareness, then you may be realizing that what you thought you wanted is only a mirage. However, the good news is that the true oasis you seek may be closer than you thought. You may be on an instinctive track toward what your heart truly desires even as you experience a season of discontent chasing what others have placed before you. When you invest in your own unique instinctive success, you will find that you don't have to chase awards, affluence, or achievements. They will find you!

INSTINCT BASICS

1. How do you presently measure and define your own personal success? What have you achieved or acquired in your life so far that's proof of your advancement? How does this evidence satisfy your instinct to increase? How does it inspire you to greater things?

_____

_____

_____

2. What achievements or apparent successes have disappointed you or left you longing for more than what you attained? How have these disappointments influenced your definition of success?

_____

_____

_____

3. What accomplishment, achievement, or work-in-progress has brought you the most personal satisfaction? What did you enjoy most about pursuing this goal? What did this pursuit bring out in you that other pursuits of success usually do not?

_____

_____

_____

Instinct Multiplies Success

Jesus' parable of the talents remains one of the most relevant, insightful applications of instinctive success that I've ever encountered. While it's symbolically spiritual in its message, it's also highly practical and applicable to virtually all areas of our lives. In many ways, it's a variation of another biblical truth, "You reap what you sow" (see Galatians 6:7). However, Jesus takes this cautionary tale about investments, consequences, and dividends one step further in the parable of the talents.

In this story of a master going on a journey, we must choose our response to a universal and fundamental question of existence: What will we do with the treasure God has invested in us? And here in the parable, we really only have two responses. We either invest boldly and wisely and return more to the master than what he originally gave us. Or, we succumb to our fears and bury our treasure, returning no dividend on our master's investment, only the original capital.

The two servants who invested their master's money, or talents as they're aptly called in Scripture, achieved an amazing promotion. "Well done, my good and faithful servant," the master says to them (Matthew 25:21, paraphrased). "You're going to be placed in charge of more! Get your things, you're coming to stay with me." As I explain in Chapter 11, this notion was entirely radical for Jesus' audience! Slaves becoming masters? What in the world could God be communicating about the nature of risking what we've been given?

On the other hand, the third servant failed in a way from which he could not recover. His plight reminds us of the ultimate regret, living a life in which we buried what we were entrusted to invest. Paralyzed by fearful, false perceptions of his master, this slave is called wicked and condemned for his tepid decision to play it safe. Yes, it seems clear that we have all been given an instinct to increase—it's only a matter of will we use it?

MORE ABOUT INSTINCTS

1. How familiar are you with this parable of the talents in Matthew 25:14-29? What new theme or implication emerged from reading it within the context of my instinctive explication?

_____

_____

_____

2. What fears influence you to bury your talents rather than invest them? What are you afraid of happening if you risk fulfilling your own God-given potential? Are you more scared of success or more afraid of failing?

_____

_____

_____

3. In what area of your life do you presently need to dig up your buried treasure and invest it in something that can produce divine dividends? What have you been holding back that you instinctively need to release at this time in your life?

_____

_____

_____

INSTINCTIVE WISDOM

"I have seen so many people who wasted their life, their gifts, their money, and all types of opportunities because fear blocked the path to abundance. Like a roadblock on a highway, they seemed unable to get beyond the debris of past accidents in order to find a new route to their success. We can overcome our fears if we remember that life does not demand more than what it gives. We're not called to use others as the barometer of our breakouts. We're called to maximize the fullness of what God has uniquely entrusted to us!"—INSTINCT, p. 124

Instincts may at first appear to be random emotional occurrences that come without thinking. Yet they are informed, though often even fleetingly, by our views of God, history, deeply held values, aspirations for the future, and our concern or lack of concern for people around us.

For that reason we explore these biblical characters whose instincts can provide lessons for us.

Matthew 25:14-30

CONSIDER THE THREE SERVANTS IN THE PARABLE OF THE TALENTS. Each was given responsibilities by his master before he left on an extended trip. One was given five thousand dollars, another two thousand dollars, and the third got one thousand dollars. These amounts depended on their abilities. The first servant immediately went to work and doubled his master's investment, as did the second. The man with the one thousand buried his master's money.

1. What was each servant's view of God based on what they did?

_____

_____

2. What experiences might each have had in their past that led to their decision?

_____

_____

_____

3. What did the three servants consider about their own future?

_____

_____

_____

4. What might each servant have considered about their family as indicated by their actions?

_____

_____

_____

5. What lessons can we learn about instinct from a consideration of each servant's decision?

_____

_____

_____

Threshold of Success

Fear is a funny thing. It can paralyze you or it can motivate you. It can detach and derail you from your instinctive direction, or it can heighten the urgency and sensitivity of your instincts. Fear remains an inevitable part of life. Even the most courageous, brave, powerful, and valiant individuals get afraid at times. No, the fear experienced by the third slave in the parable is not the problem. It's his response to the fear that caused his failure.

Our fears will always attempt to infiltrate our insight and poison our potential. But we must acknowledge them without allowing them to determine our actions. I'm convinced the more we're in touch with our instinctive drive, the more powerfully we can overcome our fears. Our instincts know that if our fears are left unchecked they can destroy us, which goes against our strongest drive to survive.

You know in your heart of hearts that you were made for more than what you've achieved so far in life. Whether you're a beggar or a billionaire, you remain poised on the threshold of instinctive success. Don't bury the treasure you've been given because you're afraid of losing it. Ironically, the only way not to lose it is to invest it in something eternal—the fulfillment of your divine destiny. Take the next risk that must be taken to be a good steward of the treasure already inside you. The greatest satisfaction comes from the achievement of what God has created you and you alone to do on this earth. He's given you powerful instincts as your guide—it's time you unleashed them for the maximum return on His investment!

INSTINCTS IN ACTION

1. When was the last time you felt the exhilaration of doing what you know you were uniquely created to do? What were the circumstances in this moment? What role did your instincts play in experiencing this kind of soul satisfaction?

_____

_____

_____

2. In your Instinct Guidebook, make a list of the talents, abilities, skills, and unique experiences you've discovered, developed, and accumulated in your life. Give each category a column and jot down as many in each category as you can.

After you're satisfied with your lists for each—talents, abilities, skills, and unique experiences—evaluate how each category is currently being invested.

3. Choose someone you trust who knows you well, preferably for a long time. Schedule some time with this confidant and discuss your fears about the future with them. Let your friend know your thoughts and feelings in response to reading INSTINCT and discovering more about yourself through this Workbook. Ask them to repeat back to you what they've heard you saying. Discuss with them anything that seems inaccurate or surprising.

"It's time for you to respond to the rapping fist of opportunity's fierce knock on the door of your life right now. If you will answer the knock and honor the chance with discipline, creativity, and urgency, you may find yourself—your true self—living a life that exceeds your wildest dreams!" (INSTINCT, p. 131).

NOTES

_____

_____

_____

_____

_____

_____

_____

_____

Protection
from Predators

Once you've taken a leap of faith and made a bold move, it's tempting to think that you've arrived at the next level. While you should celebrate your entrance into excellence, you must also be prepared to defend yourself and your core identity and beliefs as you encounter new people in your new environment. Regardless of how kind, friendly, and helpful they may appear, others will accurately regard your arrival as a catalyst for change. With their best assumptions, you strike them as a curiosity that requires further scrutiny. At their worst, the expectations of your new community members will assess you as a threat to their own instinctive success.

Just as my Roman Cane Corso dogs, Bentley and Sable, learned the hard way that their new domain included prior inhabitants, you must engage with the new people around you without assuming the worst. You don't want to get off on the wrong foot because you're automatically projecting a defensive, accusatory attitude. But on the other hand, you don't want to let your guard down all at once. You want to lower the gate to your vulnerable self gradually and slowly, over time as you get better acquainted with your new environment and its other inhabitants.

INSTINCT BASICS

1. When you find yourself in new situations, how do you usually respond to new acquaintances? How would others describe their first impressions of you? Warm and friendly? Aloof and reserved? Direct and no-nonsense? Casual and collegial?

   _____

   _____

   _____

2. Do you tend to err on the side of trusting people too much or not trusting them enough? How long does it typically take you to form an opinion or assessment of new people in your life?

   _____

   _____

   _____

3. How accurate are your first impressions of other people? What role do your instincts play in forming these initial ideas of others' character and personalities? Would you say that your instinctive assessment of others based on first impressions tends to be accurate most of the time, some of the time, or none of the time?

_____

_____

_____

Prey for Your Predators

When you arrive in a new environment, whether it be a new workplace, committee at church, or community softball team, you enter into an atmosphere already infused with alliances and opinions, history and heresy, attitudes and outlooks. Others may welcome you, enlist your support, or leave you cold, but everyone you encounter will definitely be analyzing and assessing you the same way you are sizing them up. It's simply human nature to try to find our place when introduced into a new social system. Animals, of course, are the same way—sniffing each other, barking and biting, chasing and chewing—and sometimes much more!

The difference, however, is that animals typically do not pretend to regard each other one way and then act in the opposite manner. There's no pretense, deception, or subterfuge in the animal kingdom the way we encounter it in humanity! So we must hone our instincts in ways that help us discern others' motives, methods, and machinations the same way my dogs sniff the scent of a coyote on our property.

Obviously, the more time we spend together, the more data we have to assess these new members of our society. However, here more than anywhere, don't discount your instincts. If someone strikes you as untrustworthy, even though you have no basis for it, don't tell them anything you don't want repeated! Listen to your instinctive wisdom as it filters and familiarizes you with this new cast of characters in your life's latest chapter.

MORE ABOUT INSTINCTS

1. When was the last time you were aware of being the "newbie" on the scene? What were the circumstances that led to your arrival? What were your first impressions of those around you?

_____

_____

_____

2. How would you describe your style of relating to other people? Look at the following pairs of words and choose the one in each pair that more accurately describes your relational style.

Introvert	Extrovert
Loud	Soft-spoken
Opinionated	Reserved
Analytic	Empathic
Gullible	Cynical
Conversational	Professional
Warm	Distant
Complicated	Transparent
Laid-back	Assertive
Black-and-white	Shades of grey

3. How do you usually respond when it's clear that others are evaluating you? Do you like to show off or do you tend to retreat and surprise them later? Do you resist their attempts to interrogate you or sidetrack them with stories?

_____

_____

_____

INSTINCTIVE WISDOM

"Whenever you arrive on the shores of a new career, vocation, or aspiration, you always arrive as an immigrant. You have a different scent on you and all the animals know it! What looks like a backyard when you stepped into it, will always have eyes glaring in the shadows, and native noses to the air, catching the scent of the outsider who now has changed the balance in the backyard. No amount of kindness can alter the fact that the other animals in your new world feel threatened by your arrival—which means you must be prepared to do some sniffing as well!"—INSTINCT, p. 137

Instincts may at first appear to be random emotional occurrences that come without thinking. Yet they are informed, though often even fleetingly, by our views of God, history, deeply held values, aspirations for the future, and our concern or lack of concern for people around us.

For that reason we explore these biblical characters whose instincts can provide lessons for us.

Acts 14:1-7

CONSIDER PAUL AND BARNABAS. Traveling to the city of Iconium, they went to speak at the synagogue, the Jewish meeting place. Many people believed their message of the Gospel but others started a whispering campaign, causing suspicion and mistrust of them. When they learned of a plan by their opponents to beat them up, they escaped to the next town and successfully continued their work.

1. What was Paul and Barnabas' view of God that led them to do the work they did?

_____

_____

_____

2. What might they have recalled in their history that instinctively led them to continue their work?

_____

_____

_____

3. What confidence could they have about their future as they continued their work in the next towns?

_____

_____

_____

4. What did the response of the people they reached reveal to them about God's purpose for them?

_____

_____

_____

5. What lessons can we learn from their response to the opposition and successes they encountered?

_____

_____

_____

Instinctive Identity

Thrust into the dynamics of a new social environment, it's only natural to want to fit in and be accepted. However, you must be aware of the cost. Having lunch with one group may unknowingly alienate another. Assisting certain team members may unintentionally set a precedent for how you will relate to one another. Spend some time laying low and observing the lay of the land before you begin making alliances and creating patterns in your social structure.

You will also have to make sure you remain firmly aware of your true identity as you assimilate into new jungles and jurisdictions. If you're not in possession of your instinctive strengths, abilities, and limitations, then you will soon be following someone else's script for your role. Without realizing it, you will discover yourself acting outside of character, saying what others want to hear or doing what they expect to be done.

While it's good to be accepted and respected, you want to make sure that it's for the right reasons. Doing whatever it takes just to fit in rarely earns anyone's respect in the long run. However, knowing your authentic self and asserting your instinctive identity in naturally confident ways will always command others' respect, if not their acceptance as well. Trusting your instincts remains one of the best ways to defend yourself against the pursuit of predators—just ask Bentley and Sable!

INSTINCTS IN ACTION

1. How would you describe your role or persona in each of the following social environments? Write down the first words that come to mind for all that apply.

Home: _____

Work: _____

Church: _____

School: _____

Community/Neighborhood: _____

Club or Team: _____

Other: _____

2. When have you felt attacked, betrayed, or preyed upon by others in a new environment? How did you handle such predatory behavior? How will you handle it the next time you experience a similarly hostile environment?

_____

_____

_____

3. How has your identity been challenged in your present roles and responsibilities? Which arenas seem to be the most difficult in maintaining your authentic self?

_____

_____

4. Choose one or two quotations from your readings in INSTINCT or this Workbook and write them in your Instinct Guidebook as reminders to be true to your instinctive identity. If you have other meaningful quotations from the Bible, historical figures, or instinctively successful individuals, write them in your Guidebook as well.

_____

_____

_____

"If you lose your sense of who you are, you have nothing to which you can return. If you don't discover your passions, purpose, and power, then you will pursue the roles assigned by other people's scripts. You will lose the success afforded by new opportunities if you don't know your own priorities and preferences" (INSTINCT, p. 141).

NOTES

_____

_____

_____

_____

_____

_____

_____

_____

_____

_____

_____

_____

_____

Informed
Instincts

Before you begin: Please familiarize yourself with *Chapter 13* of INSTINCT, pp. 145-153.

As we've seen, our instincts operate most accurately and effectively when they combine our external data with our internal filters of emotion, experience, and expectation. When we rely on either sector exclusively—facts without feelings or instincts without info—we severely limit our instinctive ability to succeed. Life constantly provides us with information, and at times we feel overwhelmed by all the options, opinions, and operations competing for our attention. Simply put, we can't take it all in nor should we try.

One of the great advantages of living instinctively is allowing your internal wisdom to filter and sort information for you. Many neurologists and psychologists have observed the way our brain's reticular activating system (RAS), a collection of nuclei performing many complex transitions, becomes stimulated when we encounter something that interests us. It's that experience you've probably had where you're trying to decide which car to buy, and suddenly all you notice on the highway is the model you want to purchase. It's why some articles in a magazine catch your attention and engage your thoughts while you skip over others altogether.

There's much more that could be explored about the fascinating ways our minds and bodies work harmoniously with our instincts. However, for our purposes, simply recognize that part of what makes your instincts so powerful is their ability to synthesize a variety of source information, including ones that we might not consciously recognize as sharing common elements or relationships. When we inform our instincts, we provide fuel for the passions, desires, and dreams burning within us. Make sure you don't neglect the significance of what you can learn from the facts—not just the information they impart but how they relate to all the other areas of your instinctive knowledge.

INSTINCT BASICS

1. What sources usually provide you with the most factual information? Which digital sources—websites, blogs, news sites, and forums—do you frequent most often? How reliable or trustworthy are these sources? What's the basis for their authority and credibility?

_____

_____

_____

2. Why do these particular sources that you listed above appeal to you more than other similar sources that basically provide the same information? Are there certain styles, techniques, graphics, or audio effects that engage you more than others?

_____

_____

_____

3. What other sources of information, news, and interviews do you usually use? Which magazines, periodicals, and journals? Which TV or radio news programs, talk shows, and inspirational series?

_____

_____

_____

Get Your Bearings

In order to inform your instincts, you must know what you need to know. You must be able to examine your areas of knowledge and identify ones that require more information. Or, you might need to update educational expertise that you already possess. Most professions require us to stay up-to-date with the latest developments, products, trends, and methods in our field. In order to function effectively, our instincts need the same kind of ongoing informational input.

Also, as you get your bearings by recognizing your limitations and boundaries, keep in mind that your instinctive education is dynamic and ever evolving. You never arrive and stop learning. There's never going to be a point where you have mastered any subject so perfectly that there's nothing left to discover. The areas of interest that truly attract and engage us will only continue to deepen our passion. This explains why the best experts are often those people who realize that the more they learn, the more there is to learn!

MORE ABOUT INSTINCTS

1. What educational experiences have had the greatest impact on your instincts? What training has proven to be the most valuable on a daily basis?

_____

_____

_____

2. Imagine that an intern or apprentice is shadowing you throughout your day. What would this student learn about what you do that cannot be taught in the classroom? What wisdom or advice would you pass along to this person about how to be successful?

_____

_____

3. In what areas do you want to learn more? What educational areas, job training, and professional development skills in your repertoire need updating?

_____

_____

_____

INSTINCTIVE WISDOM

"Relying on your instincts is not enough. You might survive but you won't thrive without due diligence and the research needed to sharpen and hone your instincts. I'm convinced instincts operate most accurately when they have as much data as possible. Our instincts then process the facts, figures, and financials through the filters of our personalities, experiences, and goals. It's where art and science meet to create this most unique navigational system for living."—INSTINCT, p. 145

Instincts may at first appear to be random emotional occurrences that come without thinking. Yet they are informed, though often even fleetingly, by our views of God, history, deeply held values, aspirations for the future, and our concern or lack of concern for people around us.

For that reason we explore these biblical characters whose instincts can provide lessons for us.

Numbers 13:28-33

CONSIDER CALEB and the rest of the men sent to scout out the Promised Land, Canaan. They were told by Moses to examine the land, the people, the towns, the produce, and more. Although 12 men were sent out, only Caleb and Joshua brought back a positive report. Their instincts showed them something completely different than the others saw.

1. What did Caleb's report show about his consideration of God?

_____

_____

_____

2. What historical experience could Caleb have recalled in the wilderness that informed his instincts about the land?

_____

_____

_____

3. What might Caleb have considered for his people and family when he saw the produce and bounty of the land?

_____

_____

_____

4. What differed in Caleb's view of God's purpose for the people compared to the other scouts who saw the land?

_____

_____

_____

5. What lessons can we learn about instinct from a consideration of Caleb's report? What lessons can we learn when we consider the others' report?

_____

_____

_____

Study Your Own Habits

We each have our own learning styles, and being aware of how you assimilate information most effectively is crucial to your instinctive education. If you know you don't have the patience to scrutinize financial data, then you need to find a way to extract that information in other ways. If you know that reading reports makes you fall asleep, then you need another method of grasping the facts and findings. If you know you need graphics, graphs, charts, and other visuals, then let those around you know your preference. If hearing reports explained in a conversation helps you comprehend more efficiently, then find someone who can converse.

When you know your own instinctive habits, you liberate yourself to work more effectively. Are you a night owl and get energized after dinner? Do you work best as the sun comes up and find yourself drained by mid-afternoon? Knowing the environmental factors that affect our educational success is also crucial. You want to maximize your opportunities to learn by controlling the variables within your reach. Don't underestimate the power of your learning environment. Colors, sounds, lights, movement, and texture all have an impact on how we engage and process information. Discover what works best for you and use it to your advantage.

INSTINCTS IN ACTION

1. How would you describe your learning style? Visual? Audial? Hands-on? A combination? When have you enjoyed learning the most? What factors contribute to our positive learning experience?

_____

_____

_____

2. Imagine that you have a huge report to write and present to a room full of prospective clients. Assuming you had all of the informational resources you needed, what would your ideal learning environment look like? Be as specific as possible: What color are the walls? Music (and what kind) or silence? Others working nearby or far away from anyone else? Sitting? Standing? Laying down? Windows opened or closed? Focusing on such minute details may seem silly or irrelevant, but if you pay attention to what works best for you, it's surprising how easily you can often control and manipulate these variables and improve your retention, comprehension, and performance.

3. In your Instinct Guidebook, make a list of topics, ideas, people, places, and events that you would like to know more about for whatever reason or no reason other than your own curiosity. Choose one, either the most useful or the most intriguing, to begin researching right away. Do more than an online search. Visit a library, bookstore, classroom, or museum. Find an expert if possible and ask them to explain their passion for what you're researching.

4. Using images you find online, as well as in magazines, greeting cards, art prints, and other creative sources, look for elements of your ideal learning environment, a special room that's yours alone. Whether you call it a study, office, lounge, or library, choose colors, designs, and details that would facilitate your greatest instinctive education. Now paste, sketch, draw, and paint these different elements into your Guidebook. Bonus points if you can put all the details together so that they actually look like your Dream Room!

5. What course do you need to take, which test do you need to pass, how much training do you need to sharpen your instincts in the area of your greatest passion? Take one action toward acquiring this instinctively essential information.

"If you don't find a way to enhance your instinct through research, you forfeit the opportunity to belong" (INSTINCT, p. 150).

Instinctive
Leadership

Before you begin: Please familiarize yourself with *Chapter 14* of INSTINCT, pp. 155-182.

When you live instinctively, the opportunity for leadership will naturally present itself. As you move closer to your dreams and instinctive success, you will take on more responsibilities as your endeavors expand and reach fruition. Sooner or later, you will need to enlist others in the process of fulfilling your instinctive desires and that requires leading them forward as only you can. Eventually, you look up and realize that everyone else is looking at you for direction!

Many people are intimidated by the notion of considering themselves leaders. I've found, however, that they're often more afraid of misperceptions of what they believe is required of a leader than what they may already be doing! Sometimes we assume leaders must have all the answers, be comfortable speaking before large groups, and know how to dress like an executive out of Vogue or GQ. These stereotypical qualities are rarely what determine an effective, instinctively successful leader, however.

Instinctive leaders know that ultimately it's not how they look, sound, or even what they may say. Instinctive leadership is about taking responsibility for the fulfillment of your goals. This instinctive achievement may require collaboration, synchronization, and delegation with three people or three thousand—in fact, the more successfully you progress, the more these relational components may multiply. But regardless of how big or how successful they become in pursuit of their dreams, instinctive leaders know how to remain focused. Sure, they may stray and explore new jungles that lead nowhere from time to time—after all, instinctive leaders take risks—but most of the time they're keenly focused on what they do best. Why? Because their instincts are guiding them in how they guide others!

INSTINCT BASICS

1. Do you usually think of yourself as a leader? In all arenas or just certain ones? In which areas do you feel most comfortable leading others? How much experience have you had leading in these areas?

_____

_____

_____

2. What intimidates or frightens you most about leading other people? What do you enjoy most about it? Why?

_____

_____

_____

3. Who are the leaders you've served who have had the greatest impact on you and your leadership style? What did you learn from them? How has it influenced the way you lead others?

_____

_____

_____

Tradition vs. Innovation

One of the fundamental tensions every leader faces, both within themselves and their organizations, emerges in the clash of tradition and innovation. Instinctive leaders learn quickly that they must walk the tightrope between these two foundational pillars of sustained success. On one end of the spectrum, you must acknowledge and respect what has occurred prior to your arrival in a new arena. And on the other end, you must be willing to risk doing things very differently in order for advancement and healthy growth to take place. This tension applies to virtually every area, from the people you lead (and let go) to the clients you serve and the methods you utilize.

If you want to make sure that you never achieve more than what you've accomplished presently, then keep doing things the exact same way. And if you want to make sure there's a legacy remaining beyond your leadership, then don't take any risk that jeopardizes the foundational focus of your enterprise. Instinctive leaders know that you can't ignore either of these parallel pillars supporting the foundation of your organization.

Therefore, these inherent tensions require you to discover an instinctive rhythm that accommodates both partners. Understanding tradition is often vital to identity, purpose, and continuity. If you don't grasp the essence of your brand, then you can't expand it and move it forward. Yet pursuing innovation is just as vital in the areas of relevance, progress, and growth. If you remain where you are, you soon grow stagnant and decay, going backward instead of forward. Your instincts can help you negotiate with both tradition and innovation, remaining aware of the changing needs and adapting at the right time.

MORE ABOUT INSTINCTS

1. As a leader, are you pulled more toward maintaining tradition or pursuing innovation? Does your default setting tend to leave something alone as long as it's working? Or do you like to explore change just to see if you can make things even better?

_____

_____

2. When have you felt squeezed between tradition and innovation? How did you handle the pressure? How did this experience influence your leadership instincts?

_____

_____

_____

3. What's one thing you'd like to change in the current domain of your leadership? What has prevented you from changing it already? What's one thing you would like to ensure remains the same in the present arena where you lead? How can you protect it moving forward?

_____

_____

_____

INSTINCTIVE WISDOM

"Honing your instinct for creative change at the right time sharpens the instincts of those around you. In this regard, leading by instinct can become contagious. If the people you retain don't respond to that retention and reward it with an earnest effort to remain relevant, then it backfires. The onus rests upon the team to avail themselves of all available opportunities supplied to stay cutting edge. While the company can identify training, the persons who are a part of the team share some serious responsibility not to become inflexible or irrelevant by virtue of thinking that a good relationship and personality will cover a poor performance."—INSTINCT, p. 160

Instincts may at first appear to be random emotional occurrences that come without thinking. Yet they are informed, though often even fleetingly, by our views of God, history, deeply held values, aspirations for the future, and our concern or lack of concern for people around us.

For that reason we explore these biblical characters whose instincts can provide lessons for us.

I Kings 3:4-28

CONSIDER SOLOMON. He prayed for an understanding heart once he became leader of Israel. God granted his request and when he was required to judge which of two women was the true mother of a baby they both claimed, he was able to correctly judge who was telling the truth.

1. What did Solomon's prayer show about his consideration of God?

_____

_____

_____

2. What historical examples from his own life or his father David's life might Solomon have considered?

_____

_____

_____

3. What might Solomon have considered about his future?

_____

_____

_____

4. What did Solomon reveal about his view of his people?

_____

_____

_____

5. What lesson can we apply to our leadership when we consider the decision Solomon had to make?

_____

_____

_____

Instinctive Leaders Lead

In order to lead instinctively, you must be aware of your natural default tendencies and preferences in how you make decisions, communicate them, and work with team members for their implementation and execution. As I share in this chapter, my own style of leadership is what I call consultative. I like consulting as many stakeholders as possible as well as informing my decisions with as much factual data as possible. I have no problem being decisive, but I tend to move at my own instinctive pace rather than be pressured to draw premature conclusions.

No one leadership style is necessarily better than another. Each and every unique style can work well when harnessed to a talented, hard-working individual's instincts. All styles include certain strengths and advantages as well as weaknesses and blind spots. Let's quickly review the kinds of leaders I list in this chapter in INSTINCT:

Autocratic Style: controlling, independent, decisive, forceful, confident, responsible

Chaotic Style: empowering, accessible, team-oriented, conversational, unpredictable

Democratic Style: unifying, invested, equitable, proactive, respectful

Laissez-faire Style: motivating, visionary, progressive, preoccupied, detached

Persuasive Style: captivating, charming, charismatic, personal, communicative

Strong instinctive leaders often possess many of these characteristics in some form of hybrid style. They use their instinctive sensibilities to know which qualities are needed to produce the desired results at which time. These leaders know that you must adapt and step outside your natural tendencies in order for others to invest in your mission and follow you.

When you lead instinctively, you also know that you will have to become adept at reading between the lines. From resumes to quarterly reports, often the most important messages emerge from what is not on the page. Many social skills and personality strengths will not be reflected on an applicant's resume. Budget reports and marketing updates need to be translated into more accessible language for various stakeholders.

You simply can't reduce instinctive leadership to a standard formula or a series of steps. Leading successfully requires a keen awareness of your instincts, a willingness to trust in their wisdom, and the courage to risk taking full responsibility. As you develop into a more instinctive leader, look for opportunities to stretch your abilities and follow where your instincts lead. You might be surprised how many others will follow!

INSTINCTS IN ACTION

1. In your Instinct Guidebook, make a list of the leaders you admire and respect the most. Consider various areas of your life and community, not just your workplace. Include government leaders, church leaders, historical leaders, military leaders, industry leaders, leaders of social change, and personal mentors. Make note of any common denominators that they all share in their leadership styles.

2. Which of the leadership styles listed describes your own style most accurately? As you can see, each one incudes numerous strengths as well as an area of struggle. What do you see as your greatest leadership attributes? What areas need improvement?

3. Choose someone from your list of admired leaders, probably someone local that you know, and make an appointment with them. Let them know that you admire the way they lead and want to learn from them. Think through at least three questions you want to ask them during your meeting.

4. Choose a famous, well-known, or historical leader from your admired leaders list and read a biography of this person. Make notes in your Instinct Guidebook about this person and what surprises you about their life. In what ways are you already like this instinctive leader?

"Inspirational leaders ignite a spark within us that compels us to be part of the blaze they are lighting. When you inspire people to come on board with you, you are evolving into an instinctive leader" (INSTINCT, p. 170).

NOTES

_____

_____

_____

_____

_____

_____

_____

_____

_____

_____

_____

_____

_____

_____

_____

_____

_____

_____

Instincts Don't Stink!

Before you begin: Please familiarize yourself with *Chapter 15* of INSTINCT, pp. 183-191.

Instinctive wisdom often emerges in the strangest places! As I share in this chapter, I was astounded at the insight emerging from the enormous pile of elephant excrement we encountered on my South African safari. Apparently, if you know what you're looking for, there's a wealth of information there! The animal's diet, general health, age, weight, and location can all be discerned by examining the rather unpleasant present he leaves by the wayside.

I suspect our past behavior, especially our mistakes, is just as revealing. Maybe you've heard the saying, "Your best decisions have gotten you to where you are right now." It's one I've heard said when someone expresses their dissatisfaction with their current status, meaning that decisions have played a part—a large part—in arriving at their present destination. Many life circumstances are certainly beyond our control, but how we respond to them is well within our instinctive grasp.

While our instincts aren't always accurate, rarely do they lead us astray. They're used to turning the decisions, failures, and disappointments of life into opportunities. And if we're willing to sift through the painful areas of our lives, the tender areas where we continue to feel vulnerable, then our instincts can help us heal and move forward much more quickly and effectively.

INSTINCT BASICS

1. What personal mistake or bad decision has provided you with the most insight into your weaknesses? What prompted you to make this mis-step at the time? Whether it was last week or years ago, as you look back now, what have you learned about yourself from this messy experience?

_____

_____

_____

2. How much responsibility do you take for your choices and actions in life? When you're honest with yourself, do you allow yourself to play the victim? Or do you embrace the options you do have, regardless of how limited they may be, and make the most of moving forward?

_____

_____

3. What's one mistake you've made that's turned out to have a silver lining? How has it influenced your instinctive choices since?

_____

_____

_____

Mistakes into Motivations

The wounds of our past failures often motivate us more than we realize. We become fixated on what we did wrong, blaming ourselves and blaming others, becoming bitter instead of better. Instead of learning as much as we can from these discouraging incidents, we end up getting trapped in them. We wonder why we cannot seem to move forward and yet we continue to cling to something that happened a long time ago.

As a result of our bitterness, regret, and disappointment, we run away from present opportunities rather than risk experiencing the same outcomes. Or, we refuse to look at our motives, emotional baggage, and needs and find ourselves repeating patterns that only leave us stuck, basically repeating past mistakes. We may instinctively know that in order to truly heal and move forward we must take responsibility for what we can and release what's beyond our control.

Many people ask me why they seem to be attracted to the same kind of person over and over again, always with the same painful results. Investors and entrepreneurs will sometimes inquire why I think they continue to struggle, fail, and have to start again. Individuals battling addictions also know this feeling, a sense of being caught in a cycle of futility, frustration, and failure from which they cannot find a way to escape.

It's never easy, but our instinctive desire to survive and to thrive can help us break these patterns if we let them. But we must be willing to step back and look at those messes and mistakes with a more objective, critical perspective. We must be willing to look within and assess what needs are going unmet—as well as what payoff we're getting for remaining trapped in this cycle.

God has gifted His human creations with intellect, insight, and instinct so that we can be higher than the animals. He has instilled a spiritual dimension, which we often call a soul, as an integral part of our being. We don't have to keep repeating the mistakes of the past, running from our painful mistakes, or spinning our wheels in frustration. If you use your instincts as a tool, much like a scientist uses a microscope, you can see beyond the surface and make lasting changes in the right direction.

MORE ABOUT INSTINCTS

1. Identify the major wounds that have been inflicted on you by others—your parents, family of origin, spouse, children, teachers and coaches, close friends and business associates. How have you pursued forgiveness and healing from these setbacks? What have you learned about yourself from these injuries to your soul?

_____

_____

_____

2. Identify the major wounds that you have inflicted on others—perhaps some of the same people who have hurt you deeply as well. Who do you still need to ask for forgiveness? What other lingering effects and consequences must be addressed before you are free to move forward?

_____

_____

_____

3. What incidents, accidents, and events in your life embarrass you or cause you the most shame? What secret are you holding that continues to short-circuit your instinctive drive for success? What needs to happen for you to break free of the hold these areas have on your life?

_____

_____

_____

INSTINCTIVE WISDOM

"People who have not developed their instincts waste potential and lack tenacity. I see people wasting potential every day because they lack the determined drive to develop their opportunities. To him whom much is given (favor), much is required (tenacity). When the gift is given, you must reinforce your instincts with determination and perseverance. Often our drives and tenacity come from the places that stink in our lives. The sweet smell of success is often preceded by the sour stench of past mistakes!"—INSTINCT, p. 185

Instincts may at first appear to be random emotional occurrences that come without thinking. Yet they are informed, though often even fleetingly, by our views of God, history, deeply held values, aspirations for the future, and our concern or lack of concern for people around us.

For that reason we explore these biblical characters whose instincts can provide lessons for us.

Jonah 3:1-10

CONSIDER JONAH. He is most often remembered for his disobedience which results in him being swallowed by a great fish. But Jonah's past disobedience did not stop him from leading a successful preaching revival that saved the city of Nineveh.

1. What changed in Jonah when he heard the voice of God the second time?

_____

_____

_____

2. What does Jonah's prayer (Jonah 2) say regarding his history with God?

_____

_____

_____

3. What might Jonah have considered about his future after the response of the people in Nineveh?

_____

_____

_____

4. What lessons can we learn about our instincts when we consider Jonah's decisions?

_____

_____

_____

Making Room for Instincts to Operate

If you truly want to change your life and to experience the abundant satisfaction that comes from living instinctively, then you must be willing to examine the wreckage of past mistakes and clear the scene of the accident. Just as a car crash can block the highway for hours, our collisions often impede our ability to move forward into our destiny. Instead of doing the hard work that has to be done to clear the wreckage and begin again, we remain burdened by a past we can never change.

However, we can change the future by taking responsibility and making steps toward instinctive advancement in our present. Often this process requires that we let go of old baggage, heal from past injuries, and make room for the new growth awaiting our arrival. Sometimes we literally have to clear the clutter of the past from our lives, getting rid of items that may have once served a purpose but now only get in our way. Often there's emotional baggage that must be unpacked and released. Almost always, there are changes to be made in how we spend our time each day. We must make room for our instincts to operate if we want to heed their wisdom and break free from the prison of the past.

INSTINCTS IN ACTION

1. Have at least one conversation that you need to have in order to release yourself from past pain. It may mean asking someone you've hurt for forgiveness or granting forgiveness to someone who has hurt you. It might mean discussing an incident or event with another person who can provide you with some clues about your own behavior at the time. You may need to share a secret struggle with someone and begin the process of seeking the help you need.

2. In your Instinct Guidebook, make a list of what you consider your "worst moments" or "greatest mistakes." After you've spent a few minutes compiling your list, go back through it and indicate any positive consequences that have emerged from these painful moments. Place a star next to the items on your list for which you cannot see any positives. These areas still need to be examined, addressed, and healed before you can benefit from your instinctive power to succeed.

3. Have lunch or dinner with a close friend whom you trust. Ask them to share one of their life's mistakes and how they've processed it in exchange for your own confession. Help your friend see the way that this mistake has benefited them in at least one way; ask them to do the same with yours.

"When you burn off the clutter of busyness and leave yourself time to think and study, you may get less done but the things you do will be far more productive and ultimately more organic to what you are passionate about accomplishing" (INSTINCT, p. 190).

NOTES

_____

_____

_____

_____

Balancing
Intellect and Instinct

Before you begin: Please familiarize yourself with *Chapter 16* of INSTINCT, pp. 193-202.

Our minds crave knowledge and often prefer facts that can be attained and verified from reliable sources outside of our own abilities. Our hearts crave an intangible, often emotional connection that defies analysis but proves just as accurate as any verifiable fact. Together our heads and hearts work together to produce their offspring—our instincts. However, in order for the child to be healthy, both parents need to be as active and strongly developed as possible. We can't neglect either area and expect our instincts to be operating at full capacity.

We must perform the due diligence and research necessary to inform our decisions and actions. We must search inside ourselves for the passions, desires, and attractions that fulfill our divinely appointed potential. Together, our intellect and instincts join hands and work harmoniously to carry us toward the successful satisfaction that neither could approach alone. Keeping the necessity of this balancing act as a priority, we empower our instincts to be twice as strong.

INSTINCT BASICS

1. Are you usually led more by your head or your heart? Think of a significant recent decision that illustrates your choice.

_____

_____

_____

2. How do you usually use your intellect to provide "checks and balances" on your instincts? How do you typically filter your intellectual assessments through your instincts?

_____

_____

_____

3. What's the most challenging aspect of balancing your intellect and your instincts? How often does one tend to run ahead of the other in your experience?

_____

_____

Balancing Acts

Finding balance between our intellect and our instincts often requires us to rely on our relationships. When we include people with different points of view, different biases and preferences, and different informational angles in our conversations, we're instinctively seeking balance. If we only surround ourselves with people who reinforce what we already believe, then we're not going to strike the balanced summit we need in order to see clearly.

Similarly, we must be keenly aware of our own blind spots. Everyone has weaknesses and these must be taken into account as you find the right tempo for the dance between your intellect and instincts. You cannot ignore what you don't know and assume that it won't bite you—eventually it will! So you must bring in people, perspectives, and points of view that help you see what you yourself cannot. In football, quarterbacks know that when they turn to throw a pass, they always have a blind side. If their offensive line cannot cover this blind side by holding off defenders, then the quarterback will find himself laying on his back looking up! Without someone protecting us from what we ourselves can't see, we leave the door open to predators and manipulators. Finding balance requires coverage in a 360-degree rotation.

MORE ABOUT INSTINCTS

1. Think about the three individuals you would go to right now if you had a major decision to think through. Are these three people more similar to one another or more different from one another? What can each one uniquely contribute to your attempt to find a balance between intellect and instinct?

_____

_____

_____

2. What are your blind spots? In which areas do you tend to overlook, ignore, or underestimate important perspectives? Do your emotions sometimes blind you to the facts? Does your fear of risk cause you to take too long in making crucial decisions? What are the areas you know require additional attention as you make decisions and take actions to move forward?

_____

_____

_____

3. Who's got your back? Literally, who are the people in your life who help you see things from every angle? Are there people you need to bring in so that you have full coverage for your vulnerabilities and blind spots? Who are they?

_____

_____

_____

INSTINCTIVE WISDOM

"While instincts may be the compass that gives direction, intelligence guides the process through which that transition can be realized. No one can make great decisions if they have poor information. The greater your efforts at understanding data, the more likely you are to liberate your instincts. Whether you're forging alliances with corporations or governments, churches or clubs, investors or stockholders, you can't quantify value purely based on instinct. Data has significant placement in determining value and timing of transactions and interactions."—INSTINCT, p. 194

Instincts may at first appear to be random emotional occurrences that come without thinking. Yet they are informed, though often even fleetingly, by our views of God, history, deeply held values, aspirations for the future, and our concern or lack of concern for people around us.

For that reason we explore these biblical characters whose instincts can provide lessons for us.

Luke 10:38-42

CONSIDER MARY AND MARTHA. They welcome Jesus into their home, where Martha immediately gets busy in the kitchen. Mary, on the other hand, sits at Jesus' feet and hangs on every word He says. Martha expresses her irritation to Jesus that her sister Mary is not helping in the kitchen, only to have Jesus tell her that Mary's choice was best.

1. What was Martha's instinctive response to Jesus' presence? Compare that response to Mary's.

   _____

   _____

   _____

2. What might have been Martha's history that led to her response? How might Mary's history have differed?

   _____

   _____

   _____

3. What might each woman have considered about her future?

   _____

   _____

   _____

4. What could Mary and Martha have each considered about God's purpose for their lives?

_____

_____

_____

5. What lessons can we learn from a consideration of the different decisions each sister made?

_____

_____

_____

Instinctive Flexibility

Like a tightrope walker, trapeze artist, or experienced gymnast, you must remain agile if you are to maintain an ongoing balance between intellect and instinct. Such flexibility requires you to monitor all variables of your environment as closely as possible and to adapt accordingly. If the wind's blowing too much, don't get on the high wire! Sometimes you have to wait until the various pieces align before moving forward with an opportunity. Sometimes you have to act immediately without hesitating to seize an opportunity before it disappears. Balancing your intellect with your instincts can help you know the difference!

Preparations and projections also provide the ballast you need to maintain your agility, flexibility, and adaptability. Just as new parents wouldn't bring a baby home without making preparations ahead of time, you must ensure you have what you need ahead of time as much as possible. When you've done your homework and prepared for as many contingencies as possible, then you have the freedom to improvise. Or perhaps to be more accurate, you will have more resources with which you can improvise.

Finding balance between our ideas and inclinations, our plans and possibilities, requires a conscious awareness and respect for both your head and your heart. Factual information will always remain a valuable commodity as you seek to make decisions and execute your plans. But they only tell half the story. You must also exercise your instincts in order to know how to interpret the facts, how they compare to other pieces of information, including others' perspective on them.

Facts alone will never provide you with what you need to succeed. Nor will your instincts. Allow the two, your intellect and your instincts, to converse together frequently, regularly, and openly. They won't always align nor should they. The points of friction, conflict, or concern between them often become your most revealing insight.

INSTINCTS IN ACTION

1. In this chapter in INSTINCT, I describe two women who are both valued friends of mine even though they each have opposing opinions on most topics. Their value in helping me find balance between intellect and instincts remains invaluable. Think through two friends, acquaintances, or associates from your circle who probably come at life from very different

perspectives. Invite them both to join you for a meeting to discuss an idea you would like to develop more fully. Listen carefully to what each one has to say.

2. When have you experienced a conflict between your intellect and your instincts? How did you respond to this apparent impasse? How did you find balance between them for moving forward?

_____

_____

_____

3. Choose an area of your life where you're currently contemplating your next move. Instead of a "pros and cons" list, make an "intellect and instincts" list in your Instinct Guidebook for your possible directions going forward. Which side has more points listed, intellect or instincts? What steps do you need to take to find balance between them before taking action?

"As essential as instincts are to exploring the design of your destiny, you must not ignore the facts for the feelings!" (INSTINCT, p. 193).

NOTES

_____

_____

_____

_____

_____

_____

_____

_____

_____

_____

_____

_____

_____

Instinctive
Relationships

Before you begin: Please familiarize yourself with *Chapter 17* of INSTINCT, pp. 203-218.

We've discussed the way we need to build a supportive and effective team around us, people who move to an instinctive rhythm similar to our own. While it's not necessarily easy to find these individuals, we're often able to identify our affinity with them by our shared values, goals, and instinctive methods. However, we must also recognize that our instincts will often lead us to relationships outside our natural networks. The more we experience instinctive success in new jungles, the more we will encounter animals we may not have met before!

Sometimes these intersections can be intimidating or even frightening. But if our instincts are guiding us, they're most often fruitful. Stop to consider it for a moment: If you only remain among a homogeneous group of similarly minded individuals, then you can only advance as far as your shared overlapping abilities can take you. However, exposure and encounters with wildly diverse people can stimulate, inspire, and ignite new ideas, fresh perspectives, and additional resources.

Rather than trying to insulate ourselves or expanding our network with others similar to us, we should instinctively seek out those people who are different—sometimes radically different—than we are. This might include people from different sectors of life, other professions, unique backgrounds, and diverse cultures. Consider this analogy: When you consistently remain in the same geographic area, you soon find it so familiar that you stop paying attention. You've established its parameters and know what you're going to find around most corners. However, when you go to a place or city that you've never visited before, your senses are heightened and you notice everything! The more different this locale is from home, the more likely you are to note and appreciate the differences!

INSTINCT BASICS

1. Think through the people with whom you'll be interacting today. Are the majority of these individuals more similar to you or more different? What do you have in common with each one? What's the most striking difference you have with each one?

_____

_____

_____

2. How do you usually respond to others who are vastly different from you? Are you naturally curious? Intimidated? Afraid? Uncertain? Annoyed? Something else?

_____

_____

_____

3. What biases and prejudices are you aware of holding against others who may be different from you? How did these attitudes develop in you? What steps do you need to take in order to release them so that you become more accepting of others' differences?

_____

_____

_____

Cast Your Net

While you may sometimes feel intimidated or self-conscious when interacting with people who are different than you're used to encountering, it's also very stimulating. As we've seen, our instincts often borrow transferable ideas and associations from one field to another in order to reach innovative discoveries and inventions. Without exposure to diverse interests and varied abilities, we're limiting our instincts' ability to do what they do best. Since you can never predict where your instincts might find inspiration, you must allow yourself to stretch beyond your relational comfort zone. In fact, I recommend that you actively seek out diverse individuals with whom you can exchange ideas, explore options, and exploit mutually beneficial opportunities.

When you cast a wide net to build your network, you're opening channels that might otherwise go ignored or be dismissed. Once you begin to experience the benefits of this expansive and instinctive way to build your relationships, you'll understand why they are so vitally important to fulfilling your potential for success. Whether we realize it or not, we're limited by our backgrounds, educations, cultures, and social climates. In order to see beyond them, we must allow ourselves to engage with others who don't do things the same way we do.

MORE ABOUT INSTINCTS

1. Who is the most diverse, unique individual in your current network, someone who's very different from you in a number of ways? How did you meet this person? How would you describe your relationship with them? When was the last time you experienced a conversation with them?

_____

_____

_____

2. When have you benefited from the input of someone very different from yourself? What were the circumstances that led to this encounter? What did you learn about yourself? About the other person?

_____

_____

_____

3. When was the last time you traveled outside your usual territories and visited a new place? Whether it was a different neighborhood in your city or the countryside of a foreign country, what struck you about this different place? How did it influence your instincts upon returning home?

_____

_____

_____

INSTINCTIVE WISDOM

"Our instincts often lead us across lines to make new connections. It's wise to know where the line is, but if you only stay on your side, then it's a prison! If animals in the jungle only stayed on one side of a boundary, then they might as well be in a cage at the zoo. On the other hand, we should not just go thundering into a new territory without any sense of what we're getting into."— INSTINCT, p. 206

Instincts may at first appear to be random emotional occurrences that come without thinking. Yet they are informed, though often even fleetingly, by our views of God, history, deeply held values, aspirations for the future, and our concern or lack of concern for people around us.

For that reason we explore these biblical characters whose instincts can provide lessons for us.

Nehemiah 2:1-20

CONSIDER NEHEMIAH. He had a great job in the palace and reported directly to the king. When he learned that his home country was in ruins, he sought and gained permission, provision, and protection from the king to return to his country. He assembled a diverse team and succeeded in rebuilding the walls of Jerusalem despite intense opposition.

1. What was Nehemiah's instinct about God when he made his bold request to the king?

_____

_____

_____

2. How did Nehemiah's understanding of his own history and that of his people inform his actions?

_____

_____

_____

3. What might Nehemiah's view of his future have been if he had not acted?

_____

_____

_____

4. What could he have considered regarding his family and his people?

_____

_____

_____

5. What lessons might we learn about instinct from a consideration of Nehemiah's request and the king's response?

_____

_____

_____

Instincts beyond Borders

In order for your instincts to carry you beyond the borders of your own self-imposed barriers, you must consider the different aspects of instinctive relationships. In this chapter, I explain four important principles that can help you expand your abilities to interact with others. Let's quickly review them.

Inspiration: The differences and dissonance between what we know and what we encounter in other distinct individuals often stirs our imaginations into action. The greater the differences, the better we can see beyond our own limitations.

Intersections: We frequently cross paths with individuals who are vastly different from us. Each intersection is an opportunity for us to expand our instinctive vision and sharpen our instinctive abilities.

Integration: Once we encounter the differences of others, how do we then put what we've observed into practice? When we recognize and identify the mutual benefits, then we can pursue shared goals of instinctive action.

Execution: Regardless of who you meet or what you learn from their differences, your instinctive drive will not improve or accelerate without taking action. You must transform your inspiration, intersection, and integration into action if you want to succeed.

As you become more comfortable allowing your instincts to guide you, they will inevitably lead you beyond the familiar into new jungles of opportunity. The participants will be different, which in itself provides you with new possibilities and fresh perspectives. Don't allow fear, prejudice, or discomfort with the unfamiliar to rob you of the precious gift of instinctive relationships. Cast your nets wide and enjoy the new fish in your network!

INSTINCTS IN ACTION

1. Seek out an opportunity to encounter other people with interests, backgrounds, and priorities vastly different than your own. It might mean attending a group meeting, an ethnic cultural center, a university classroom, a barbershop or beauty parlor, or a church Bible study. Meet and mingle with as many people as possible and choose at least one with whom you exchange contact information for a follow-up meeting.

2. Explore a culture from a country other than the one in which you were born, ideally one that intrigues you that you've always wanted to learn more about. After researching online, describe what interests you about this culture and its people and customs in your Instinct Guidebook. Illustrate your description with at least one image, photo, or sketch of something unique and iconic from this culture.

3. Plan a trip that's within your budget that will take you to a place you've never visited. It might be a suburb in the area where you live or it could be an exotic locale that you've dreamed of exploring. Set a date and begin the process of preparing for this instinctive excursion.

"An instinct without execution is only a regret. We need other people—more than just the usual suspects. Extend your net and make it work in new and instinctive ways—you might be surprised what you can catch!" (INSTINCT, p. 218).

NOTES

_____

_____

_____

Juggling by Instinct

Before you begin: Please familiarize yourself with *Chapter 18* of INSTINCT, pp. 219-231.

Most people, especially if they're successful, become accustomed to juggling multiple responsibilities. With seemingly more and more to do each day, we're all encouraged to multi-task, multi-track, and multi-ply our efforts. However, as we become instinctively led, we will soon discover that not all juggling is created equal! Sometimes we're juggling the wrong balls in the air. We're taking on projects, tasks, and obligations that we instinctively know are not in our sweet spot. As uncomfortable as it may feel to disappoint others, our instincts can help us form important boundaries if we follow them.

On the other hand, our instincts will also cause us to pick up new items to juggle along the journey of pursuing our best lives. With each new opportunity and instinctive achievement, you may have more to know, see, touch, do, research, find, and execute on a daily basis. While it's certainly challenging, if it's truly instinctively directed, then your passionate satisfaction for fulfilling your life's purpose will energize and sustain you. In other words, when you're doing a lot all at once for the right reasons, juggling can be enjoyable.

INSTINCT BASICS

1. What are the areas that you're currently juggling? Which ones should you allow to drop so that you can make room for new instinctive additions?

_____

_____

_____

2. Prioritize the things you're currently juggling in your life. What responsibility is most important to you? And what's next after it? And then? Does the way you spend each day juggling reflect these priorities?

_____

_____

_____

3. What do you enjoy most about the things you're presently juggling? How are you benefiting from each one? Once again, are there some that you need to remove from your juggling routine?

_____

_____

_____

From One Jungle to the Next

Once you begin living more instinctively, you will become more adept at taking risks as well as knowing which ones to take at which times. This sense of discernment is crucial to your instinctive advancement. Again, notice how important timing, pacing, and rhythm are to following your instincts successfully. Jugglers know that they must remain focused, engaged, and active in order to keep all the chain saws in the air!

This innate sense of timing will also guide you progressively as you navigate toward your goals. Think about the old Tarzan movies and cartoons and how he would swing from vine to vine in order to traverse the jungle. Like an experienced trapeze artist, you must also keep your hands touching all significant areas, releasing some when needed to advance, and grabbing hold of the next one. Forward motion requires that you do more than simply throw things up in the air. You instinctively must know when to let go of ones that are no longer useful and when to embrace those that can serve new adaptive purposes. As one jungle of success leads to another, you will then be able to maintain your momentum and cover more ground, all without losing sight of your ultimate instinctive priorities.

MORE ABOUT INSTINCTS

1. How well are you currently juggling the various demands and responsibilities of your life? Are you moving forward or just barely keeping them up in the air? What steps do you need to take in order to advance?

_____

_____

_____

2. When have you experienced the transition from one new jungle to another? How did you handle the transition? What will you do differently the next time you make this leap?

_____

_____

_____

3. Consider a time when you know you've "dropped the ball" and let something crash to the ground amidst your juggling. What were the consequences of dropping this item? How did you recover?

_____

_____

_____

Instincts may at first appear to be random emotional occurrences that come without thinking. Yet they are informed, though often even fleetingly, by our views of God, history, deeply held values, aspirations for the future, and our concern or lack of concern for people around us.

For that reason we explore these biblical characters whose instincts can provide lessons for us.

Acts 18:1-4, 18-28

CONSIDER AQUILA AND PRISCILLA. They worked with Paul in the tent making business in Corinth. When Paul decided to leave Corinth for Syria, they went with him. But later they got off the ship in Ephesus where they met Apollos whom they taught and helped to become a more powerful evangelist.

1. How might their views of God and vocation (tent making) have affected the business relationship between Aquila, Priscilla, and Paul?

_____

_____

_____

2. What might they have recalled regarding their history?

_____

_____

_____

3. Priscilla and Aquila decided to go with Paul to Syria. In doing so, what might they have considered regarding their future?

_____

_____

_____

4. What could they have considered about their future from their encounter with Apollos?

_____

_____

_____

5. What lessons can we learn about instinct when we consider the moves and meetings of Priscilla and Aquila in this text?

_____

_____

_____

Diversify Your Dreams

Sometimes we unwittingly limit ourselves because we can't imagine juggling one more item in our day. We may falsely assume that all our endeavors require the same level of engagement, the same amount of time, or the same degree of involvement. But when you stop to think about it, you know that all the things you're juggling do not require the same things from you. While you may feel spread too thin, you may be expending more energy and investing more time in areas that are not productive or efficient with regard to your investment.

Instinctively juggling in the most productive ways requires you to look for overlapping opportunities and common denominators that can be combined. If your business model is instinctively designed, then do you need to develop a new one when you franchise your entrepreneurial endeavor?

When you find the right people for your team, then a crucial key to juggling successfully is utilizing them for maximum impact. Many others may be able to perform some of the tasks that you're juggling; these should be delegated so that you can concentrate on the areas that are instinctively unique to your fulfillment.

INSTINCTS IN ACTION

1. Review the list of responsibilities as well as priorities you made above. Flag the items you're currently juggling that are not squarely focused on your instinctive identity and advancement. Choose at least one item on your list to delegate—something you're currently doing that many others could do for you. Invest the time you gain into one of your key areas that needs more attention.

2. Identify an opportunity to enter a new jungle that you've delayed because of all you're juggling. Make a list of common denominators this new jungle has with some of the areas you're already keeping in the air. How can this new jungle fit into the mix? Where does it overlap with other important areas of your life?

_____

_____

_____

3. Look at your schedule for the next week. Cancel or postpone at least one unnecessary appointment, meeting, or event that's clearly outside your instinctive priorities. Use the added time to reconfigure the pace of juggling your other items as well as to rest and renew your energy.

_____

_____

_____

"The demands on your life don't have to be identical to be interrelated. That passion you have, the vibrancy of your intellect, the experiences you've garnered helped propel you forward like a comet, grow into a planet, and soon become a new universe" (INSTINCT, p. 231).

NOTES

_____

_____

_____

_____

_____

_____

_____

_____

_____

_____

Instincts
Adapt

Before you begin: Please familiarize yourself with *Chapter 19* of INSTINCT, pp. 233-243.

No matter how successfully we're following our instincts, we will always need to adapt to the constantly changing world around us. Whether this requires daily tweaks or annual evaluations, our goals and methods of execution will vary depending on the individual. However, change is a constant that our instincts never ignore. Therefore, we must stay attuned to the evolution of the environment around us.

Some changes will be obvious and have to be made in response to events and circumstances beyond your control. When the market shifts, when new competitors emerge, when new products launch, you know that you must take action. Even if you decide to take no action, do it deliberately and instinctively! Your own needs change over time as do the needs, goals, desires, and methods of the people around you. Living instinctively requires you to remain engaged with the present so that you can be prepared for the future.

INSTINCT BASICS

1. When was the last time you made a significant change or improvement in the way you do things? What precipitated this shift or change? What were the results of implementing this change?

   _____

   _____

   _____

2. What's one constant in the way you typically approach fulfilling your responsibilities? Do you know what you need to function at maximum capacity? Better still, do you live according to what your instincts have revealed about the way you perform most effectively?

   _____

   _____

   _____

3. When was the last time you felt unprepared for a sudden shift or change beyond your control? How did you respond to it? How have you prepared for another similar change or problem based on this experience?

_____

_____

_____

Instinctive Longevity

The example of the brontosaurus in this chapter contains a cautionary message for everyone. Unwilling to lower its neck to the foliage below its preferred tree-level nourishment, the brontosaurus apparently died because of its inability to adapt. Once its food supply diminished, it expired instead of adapting. We, too, must know when to make dramatic changes in order to survive. Whether this means relocating to another area, switching careers, investing what we've saved, saving an unexpected windfall, or forming new alliances, we must rely on our instincts or risk becoming extinct.

Just as our instincts can guide us in our daily decisions, they can also assist us as we make decisions and choose paths that have lifelong consequences. And perhaps more importantly, our instincts often serve as a bridge between the daily habits and our long-term goals. When we trust our instincts to guide us, we continually look for connections between the daily details and our divine destiny. Like a beautiful mosaic, the small pieces of our lives make up the masterpiece that will be our legacy.

MORE ABOUT INSTINCTS

1. How have your instincts shaped your long-term goals? How have your long-range instincts translated into daily habits? What corrective steps need to be taken in order to solidify the bridge between the details and the destiny, today's needs and tomorrow's triumphs?

_____

_____

_____

2. What major life-changing decision is looming on the horizon for you? It might involve ending or beginning a significant relationship, starting a family, launching your own company, switching careers, going back to school, or retiring. What are you doing today to help you make this choice?

_____

_____

_____

3. Where do you see yourself a year from now? Five years from now? How can your instincts assist you right now in achieving this destination?

_____

_____

_____

INSTINCTIVE WISDOM

"Unorthodox thinkers are creative. They deviate from the traditional to the transformative and break into new foliage by discerning the times and making the changes necessary to keep things at least the same if not better! Stiff-necked people will destroy vital opportunities because they can't adapt to trends and changes around them—they remain too intent on defining themselves by past practices. They think, 'I have never' means 'I can't evolve.' Sadly, they often end up in the valley of dry bones."—INSTINCT, p. 238

Instincts may at first appear to be random emotional occurrences that come without thinking. Yet they are informed, though often even fleetingly, by our views of God, history, deeply held values, aspirations for the future, and our concern or lack of concern for people around us.

For that reason we explore these biblical characters whose instincts can provide lessons for us.

I Samuel 25:1-42

CONSIDER ABIGAIL. Her quick response to the threat on her household resulting from a rash decision made by her husband, Nabal, saved her life and those of her servants. Abigail made an instinctive decision that not only preserved and enriched her life, it also prevented David from committing murder.

1. What is revealed about Abigail's view of God in the way and the words that she used to appeal to David?

_____

_____

_____

2. How might Abigail's instinctive understanding of David's history have informed her statements to him in I Samuel 25:29?

_____

_____

3. What might Abigail have considered regarding her future?

_____

_____

_____

4. What lessons can we learn from Abigail's example of instinctive decision making in a volatile and changing situation?

_____

_____

_____

Better Instincts, Best Practices

As we've discussed, one of the most powerful benefits of living instinctively emerges in the gift of discernment. When we have factual information and filter it through our instinctive sensibilities, we naturally become more adept at making important decisions. Often these choices create lasting, even lifelong, benefits that in turn have a domino effect on so many other areas of our lives. For instance, knowing the kind of lifestyle we ultimately desire often determines our spending habits today. You don't have to listen to your instincts to know that blowing your budget on a regular basis will sabotage the dreams you have for your future success.

Our instincts can guide us, however, toward what business gurus often call "best practices," the inherited wisdom of our predecessors applied to ongoing methods. Since we know that one size does not fit all in any situation or endeavor, then what works best for one person might not work at all for another. This reflects the beauty of our individuality and the divine creative gift of instincts to guide us. We don't have to do things like everyone else; in fact, we must forge our own path in order to fulfill the specific destiny that is ours and ours alone.

Establishing best practices must be tempered by remaining current with the changes and revised needs of evolving circumstances. Setting any rule in stone can be dangerous if we're not willing to chisel a little deeper when things change! Today's best practices may be obsolete by next year. Again, our instincts help us navigate the inherent tension between tradition and innovation, between our head and our heart, between what others want from us and what we want for ourselves. We must never become so predictable or set in our ways that we end up being a dinosaur.

INSTINCTS IN ACTION

1. Which personal habits and preferred methods need to be re-examined in order to keep them current, effective, and instinctively attuned? Are there some that you already know need to be changed in some way? What has prevented you from adapting them already?

_____

_____

_____

2. Assuming you have the same roles and responsibilities that you're presently juggling, write out your ideal schedule for a typical workday in your Instinct Guidebook. Would you rather sleep in and stay late? Go in early and leave after lunch? Work from home? Think through the instinctive knowledge you've gained about yourself and how you work best. Be as specific as possible in scheduling the various requirements of your day.

3. Look at your ideal daily schedule and compare it to what you did yesterday. How do they compare? Where are they dramatically out of sync? What changes are within your power of control to make so that you can be more productive?

_____

_____

_____

"Relearning what you thought you knew well is important in every facet of life" (INSTINCT, p. 240).

NOTES

_____

_____

_____

_____

_____

_____

_____

_____

Treetop Instincts

Before you begin: Please familiarize yourself with *Chapter 20* of INSTINCT, pp. 245-258.

As you instinctively ascend in your success, you will discover that there will almost always be others below you taking shots at you in flight. As I recount in this chapter, I learned this in a dramatic fashion thanks to two very different encounters. One involved writing a series of editorials for a prestigious publication and receiving numerous mean-spirited critiques of my ideas and their expression. The other occurred on my South African safari as I observed the elegant giraffes eating from the tender leaves of the treetops at the edge of the jungle.

The lesson I learned from these two seemingly dissimilar experiences clearly emerged as the product of my instinctive revelation. The editor who asked me to write for her publication later told me that the people criticizing me weren't even the intended audience. Many of them were not even reading what I'd written but simply raving and ranting to attract attention!

She encouraged me to ignore these kinds of uninformed, destructive critics intent on impeding my progress for whatever personal reason motivated them—anger, jealousy, frustration, envy, or something else. Constructive criticism is always welcome, even when it's hard to hear. But the naysayers who belittle you for risking new jungles should never be taken seriously, and you should never give their stinging words the power to hold you back from your instinctive progress.

INSTINCT BASICS

1. When have you been forced to contend with criticism that was unfounded, ill-informed, or simply directed (or mis-directed) at you personally? How did you handle it at the time? How would you handle it now?

   _____

   _____

   _____

2. When was the last time you received constructive criticism that enabled you to improve your endeavors and methods? What's inherently different in this kind of feedback?

   _____

   _____

   _____

3. How have you allowed the criticism of others—whether destructively or constructively intended—to prevent you from attempting new challenges? How do you usually respond to your critics? In general, are you more likely to withdraw or to engage? To defend or to attack?

_____

_____

_____

Taste the Treetops

Giraffes instinctively know that the best source of nutrients for their unique physical needs comes from the food that happens to be at their eye level. They don't attempt to eat at ground level or chest level. As a result, they usually ignore those creatures clamoring around their feet. We must do the same.

As you instinctively ascend, you will require a different diet of information and relationships. Others might not understand your growth, let alone celebrate it with you. Depending on their own maturity and instinctive awareness, they may seek to take out their own personal issues onto the canvas of your ascension. Instinctively, you will know that their remarks have very little to do with you and everything to do with their own issues. Once you recognize that this is indeed the situation, then you must not stoop and resort to their level. Don't undo your instinctive success because of the way others handle their own shortcomings! As I say elsewhere in INSTINCT, I've never met a hater who's doing better than me!

MORE ABOUT INSTINCTS

1. What are some of the changes you've made as you've become more successful in life? How have others responded to these changes? How have you handled the negative criticisms of those who clearly have hidden or personal agendas?

_____

_____

_____

2. When have you lowered yourself and tried to respond to a critic's charges? Were you able to have a productive conversation? Or more of an emotional shouting match? What did you learn from this exchange?

_____

_____

_____

3. When have you been tempted to criticize or belittle someone else's achievements or attempts at advancement? What was motivating your criticism? How do you usually handle ugly emotions—such as jealousy, resentment, and envy—when they emerge in response to the success of others?

_____

_____

_____

INSTINCTIVE WISDOM

"Once you get to a certain stature, you can't find nourishment in low places. Just because turtles dwell at your feet doesn't mean you should come down from your height and barter with, debate, or eat alongside them. As you rise, you must adjust your source of nourishment and affirmation accordingly. Yes, like the dinosaurs, there are times when you must adapt and bend your neck to eat—but only if there's no nourishment from the top!"

–INSTINCT, p. 249

Instincts may at first appear to be random emotional occurrences that come without thinking. Yet they are informed, though often even fleetingly, by our views of God, history, deeply held values, aspirations for the future, and our concern or lack of concern for people around us.

For that reason we explore these biblical characters whose instincts can provide lessons for us.

Judges 7:1-7

CONSIDER GIDEON. He started with an army of 32,000 men. Before he engaged in his famous battle, God asked him to dismiss anyone who was afraid or fearful; 22,000 went home. God then instructed Gideon to choose only 300 men from the 10,000 that remained, and it is this small band that got the victory. God will remove many from your life as you seek instinctive success.

1. What was Gideon's view of God that shaped his obedience to God's word? (See also Judges 6:11-40.)

_____

_____

_____

2. What might Gideon have recalled regarding his history with God?

_____

_____

3. What might Gideon have considered regarding his people?

_____

_____

_____

4. How did Gideon express his confidence in God's purpose for his life? (See Judges 7:15.)

_____

_____

_____

5. What lessons can we learn about instinct as we consider the decisions Gideon made?

_____

_____

_____

Feed What's Feeding You

If you want to experience instinctive growth and fulfill your God-given potential, then you must replenish the sources that provide you with nourishment. Our bodies instinctively know this—fresh blood continuously courses through our bodies as dispensed from the beating of our cardiac muscles. People who continue to explore new territories and tame new jungles know that they have to be responsible with their expansion, as stewards and not consumers.

Such replenishment also enables us to distinguish our adversaries from our allies more clearly. Those critics intent on our destruction will continually seek to sabotage the source of our instinctive power. Our allies, by contrast, will naturally collaborate with us to restore, revive, and renew the resources that feed the fire within us. When we feed what feeds us, we're ensuring ongoing nourishment for our future as well as others behind us.

Once again, we see that our instinctive wisdom is dynamic, adaptive, and creative. If we settle for status quo, if we view ourselves as takers and consumers instead of creators and contributors, then we miss out on enormous growth opportunities. And if we continue to deplete the resources that nourish us, we will eventually discover that we've missed out on the most wonderful, satisfying soul food of all—the contentment of fulfilling our destiny.

INSTINCTS IN ACTION

1. Where have you been engaging beneath your abilities with critics who are only slowing you down? Where do you need to stop fighting and start flying?

_____

_____

_____

2. In your Instinct Guidebook, write a letter to a specific person whose negative criticism has gotten under your skin. Address the specific points or mean-spirited language that upsets you the most. Tell them how you feel and conclude by letting them know that you forgive them and are moving on. From now on, you will no longer give them the power to slow down your instinctive progress.

3. Write another letter—not in your Guidebook this time since you're going to mail it—to someone who has been an encourager, a cheerleader, a coach, and sincere supporter of your instinctive advancement. Thank this person and let them know how they have made a difference in your life. Don't email or text; write this letter the old-fashioned way, showing this person they're worth the time and attention it took to compose this letter by hand.

4. Find an image of a giraffe online or in a magazine or other source. Print or cut out this image and post it in a visible place where you will see it each day—on your bathroom mirror, your car's dash, or your computer at work. Let it be a reminder to keep eating from the treetops and never to stoop to the level of any destructive detractors!

"If you want to live by instinct, feed your heart and stretch to the treetops!" (INSTINCT, p. 258).

NOTES

_____

_____

_____

_____

_____

_____

_____

_____

_____

_____

All That
Is Within You

Before you begin: Please familiarize yourself with *Chapter 21* of INSTINCT, pp. 259-268.

As our excursion into the exploration of our instincts concludes, I hope you've discovered at least a good portion of the vast treasure within you. We've examined a variety of ways that our instincts equip, empower, and enlighten us on our life's journey. My hope is that you have gained some immediate tools, tips, and techniques by which you can become more instinctively attuned to realizing the greatness within you.

However, I also hope that your instinctive appetite has been whetted to want more for your future and to know that you can do anything necessary as you advance toward fulfilling what God has called you to do. Whether you feel the confidence or not, you have been given everything you need to take the next step toward your destiny. My prayer is that somehow the message of INSTINCT and the exercises you've completed in this Workbook will stay with you for the rest of your life.

INSTINCT BASICS

1. What three insights, tools, or new ideas will you carry with you from reading INSTINCT and completing these exercises?
2. What's been most helpful throughout this process of exploring your instincts and activating them within you?
3. How have you noticed positive change since you started reading INSTINCT and working through the questions and exercises contained here? What's instinctively different about you now than when you began this process?

You Have What It Takes

Confidence comes in many forms, and often you don't realize the personal resources at your disposal. This may be due to the fact that they've never been affirmed in you or you've never had to exercise them up until now. I'm convinced so much of what our instincts have to offer us is simply the faith to trust that we will survive and we will ultimately succeed. Many days we wonder and even can't imagine how we will get out of bed and face the day. But we do! We muster the courage, the grit, the divinely instinctive resolve within us and we do the next thing that needs doing.

You have already overcome so many obstacles to reach this moment, my friend. As you pause for a moment to catch your breath on your latest summit, do not look down and doubt yourself.

Although you may still have many miles to go before you reach your ultimate goals, you have made it this far. You have not given up. You have pushed through discouragement, doubt, despair, and depression. You are a fighter, a survivor, and a masterpiece in the making!

MORE ABOUT INSTINCTS

1. What obstacles have you overcome in the past year to get to where you are now? How have you persevered? What and who has sustained you? What role have your instincts played in this process?

2. List your three greatest personal strengths—and don't be modest! How can you draw on these three assets to instinctively advance either of them?

3. Think back to a trial or difficult season in your life, a period when you weren't sure how you would keep going. What got you through that season? What did you learn about yourself from persevering? How has surviving and overcoming this time in your life become a source of courage and confidence?

INSTINCTIVE WISDOM

"Somewhere in your passions lie the clues to your deeper purpose. It is my hope that you will recognize the divine investment placed within you and garner all your resources to steward this treasure for the future before you. In short, you have what it takes! All that you need is within you and can be accessed instinctively. Understanding this truth secretes confidence, which I'm convinced has a lot to do with overcoming obstacles and releasing your inherent resilient power."
—INSTINCT, pp. 262-263

Ready, Aim, Pull

If you've completed your reading of INSTINCT, and explored the inner jungle within you for the buried treasure of your instinctive desires and abilities, then you are ready to make some bold moves! There's a reason you picked this book up in the first place. There's a reason you've pushed yourself and completed the hard work of soul searching and instinct-equipping that's taken place through your experiences in this Workbook. Even if you cannot yet identify what these bold moves might be, your instincts already know!

Don't lose your momentum. Don't make any more excuses or allow any more obstacles to impede your instinctive progress. You can feel the "urgency of now" that we discussed earlier in INSTINCT, and you know your time is at hand. Don't delay. Use what you've discovered within yourself to move to the next level. It's time to leave the cage, fly out of the nest, and soar to new heights! I wish you Godspeed on the mighty adventure that awaits!

INSTINCTS IN ACTION

1. Review what you've written and recorded in your Instinct Guidebook over these past weeks. What's been the most eye-opening discovery about yourself? How will you utilize what you've learned to live more instinctively going forward?

2. What chapters or passages have you returned to, reread, and underlined in both INSTINCT and this Workbook? What's the most important message you've received from this experience?

3. In your Guidebook, start a fresh page and list three goals that you want to pursue in the next week as a result of how you've grown, changed, and become more instinctively aware. Begin at least one of them today. The time is now so put your instincts in action!

"You have what you need when you need it! Maybe not always exactly when you want it—but when you need it" (INSTINCT, p. 260).

NOTES

_____

_____

_____

_____

_____

_____

_____

_____

_____

_____

_____

_____

_____

Appendix:

Seven Guidelines for Christian Decision Making

Wherever your instincts lead you, it is critical to realize that never will God bring you to a decision that is at odds with His will, His word, or His way. Use this guide to check your instincts and to gain assurance that the decisions you reach are God honoring and life fulfilling:

- Does Scripture explicitly prohibit the decision? (Ephesians 5:1-7; James 2:10)

- Have I devoted time to prayer humbly asking God to help me make a wise decision? (Proverbs 3:5,6; James 1:5)

- Have I sought the wisdom of Godly counselors? (Proverbs 15:22; 11:14)

- Have I carefully considered the impact on my future? (Ephesians 5:17)

- Have I thoughtfully meditated on the past decisions and their consequences? (Ephesians 6:7-10; Romans 6:17-21)

- Have I reflected on the impact on my family and close friends? (Romans 13:10)

- Does my decision honor God? (Colossians 3:17)

Instinctive Animal Evaluation

As I share throughout INSTINCT, my safari in South Africa produced many powerful insights as I encountered various native animals. Sometimes I think we may have more in common—at least instinctively—with these inhabitants of the jungle than we realize. While it's just for fun, this questionnaire will help you discover which animal you most resemble in your instinctive inclinations.

Choose the response that best expresses your answer to each question or prompt. While more than one might apply, don't think too long about your response. Just go with your first instinct!

1. **How do you most enjoy spending your weekends?**
   a. relaxing at home with no schedule
   b. catching up on projects at work
   c. attending a new art exhibit
   d. planning your next vacation
   e. going out with friends for a group activity
   f. training for a marathon

2. **Which of the following would you most enjoy watching?**
   a. documentary on public television
   b. action-suspense movie
   c. independent film with subtitles
   d. motivational speaker on YouTube
   e. fashion and design shows
   f. sports channel

3. **You would describe the way you work as:**
   a. slow and steady
   b. aggressively focused
   c. sporadic but productive
   d. always looking ahead
   e. collaborative and consistent
   f. efficient and independent

4. **How do you usually form impressions of others?**
   a. several meetings or conversations over time
   b. how they compare to you
   c. their ability to pique your curiosity
   d. how they interact with a group
   e. their ability to entertain or amuse you
   f. their punctuality and ability to keep up

5. **When making a presentation, what's your priority?**
a. giving yourself plenty of time
b. using memorable visuals to make your points
c. creating a dramatic attention getter
d. focusing on the bottom line
e. being efficient and entertaining
f. fast-pacing that covers a lot of ground

6. **Your ideal vacation would include:**
a. laying by the pool in a relaxed, sunny resort
b. adventure-themed excursions with lots of activities
c. boutique hotel in a large city overseas
d. destination location with scheduled tour of sights
e. exotic shopping excursion with close friends
f. large group guided tour with a full schedule

7. **Your family members would most likely describe you as:**
a. a careful planner who follows through on attaining goals
b. a driven, focused competitor who knows how to win
c. a quirky charmer who always surprises them
d. a natural leader who's always looking ahead
e. someone who works hard and players harder
f. a decisive quick-thinker who's constantly on the go

8. **How would you handle a conflict with your boss or supervisor?**
a. ignore the problem and keep going
b. aggressively defend your position
c. step back and take an unexpected approach
d. focus his attention on the end result or shared goal
e. diffuse the tension with charm and a dash of humor
f. reach a compromise or resolution as quickly as possible

9. **Which of the following activities or events would be your least favorite?**
a. a fast-paced dance class
b. a philosophical discussion on peace
c. a week-long conference with full schedule each day
d. completing a list of small chores at home
e. a silent personal retreat
f. a leisurely drive with no real destination

10. Most days, your wardrobe would belong in the pages of:

a. L.L. Bean catalog

b. Vogue or GQ

c. National Geographic

d. Brooks Brothers catalog

e. Marie Claire or Esquire

f. Runner's World

11. When running late and stuck in traffic, you would probably:

a. take a deep breath, relax, and turn up the radio

b. take any available alternate route to keep moving

c. drive across the median to create a shortcut

d. use phone app or computer to determine length of delay

e. call your best friend to plan lunch next week

f. call your office and delegate tasks until you arrive

12. Which of the following people do you most admire?

a. Ronald Reagan

b. Hillary Clinton

c. Pablo Picasso

d. Warren Buffett

e. Ella Fitzgerald

f. Serena Williams

13. Imagine that you have to share some bad news with a close friend. Which sounds most like you?

a. "Can we schedule some time together next week?"

b. "I've got some bad news that you need to hear."

c. "Remember the time when we had dinner at that little Italian place?"

d. "I know it's hard but look at the big picture."

e. "Let's meet the gang for dinner and talk you through this."

f. "Don't let this slow you down."

14. After receiving an unexpected promotion, you would celebrate by:

a. increasing the withholding for your 401(k) or retirement account

b. calling a team meeting to share your number one priority

c. buying a new designer briefcase

d. looking ahead at your next career move

e. meeting co-workers for drinks after work

f. moving into your new office space

15. You're most likely to trust your instincts when:

a. planning for where you want to be in five years

b. changing careers to start your own business

c. redecorating our home

d. writing the company mission statement

e. thinking on your feet to solve an unexpected problem

f. applying for a similar position with a competing company

16. If you could follow your natural pace each day, you would:

a. take your time and complete one big task

b. move slowly until motivated to expend a burst of energy

c. jump from one thing to the next, finishing some, leaving others

d. follow a schedule based on main priorities

e. cover a lot of ground based on what engages you

f. move rapidly to get as much done as possible

17. What's your favorite kind of social event?

a. a relaxed, informal dinner party with 6-8 people

b. a formal fund-raiser with lots of movers and shakers

c. an exclusive premier party for a new play

d. a professional luncheon with lots of networking

e. a big theme party with dozens of people

f. tailgating with various friends before the big game

18. How would you handle spilling coffee on yourself right before an important meeting?

a. unruffled, you'd calmly clean up the spill as best you could

b. annoyed, you'd buy a new shirt to wear instead of the stained one

c. amused, you would ask the name of the brand of coffee

d. undisturbed, you'd change into a spare shirt you keep in your office

e. embarrassed, you would make a joke about it

f. agitated, you would rinse your shirt before anyone noticed

19. Which of the following characteristics annoys you the most in others?

a. making hasty decisions before all information is known

b. having no real ambition or sense of direction

c. conforming for the sake of fitting in

d. focusing only on details and short-term solutions

e. taking life too seriously

f. moving slowly and indecisively

20. The kind of meal you would enjoy the most tends to be:

a. an unrushed homecooked dinner with family and friends

b. a catered dinner party in your honor

c. a gourmet meal at your favorite specialty bistro

d. a holiday gathering with everyone contributing

e. an impromptu barbeque with friends who just dropped by

f. a five-course meal that you've cooked yourself using new recipes

Results

Now tally your results based on the number of times you selected each lettered response (a, b, c, d, e, or f). Which letter did you choose most frequently? Correlate the letter you chose most often with its safari animal. Do you agree with your type of animal? Or are you surprised? What kind of animal would you have selected prior to taking this little survey? Although this is imprecise and just for fun, it's sometimes quite revealing!

If you most frequently chose a), you're an ELEPHANT.

Slow and steady, elephants are planners who take their time and persevere to reach large goals over time. They're often no-nonsense, practical, solid, substantive, and determined. They don't like being rushed but can surprise others with how quickly they respond when circumstances require it. Elephants usually enjoy laid-back, relaxed environments with small groups of friends and family.

If you chose b) most often, then you're a LION.

The king of beasts is an aggressive hunter, always on the prowl and eager to chase its prey. Lions are driven, ambitious, and motivated by achievement and success. They take great pride in their appearance and exude a charismatic, dynamic quality that can sometimes intimidate others. They like being the center of attention but want to earn the respect and admiration of others for who they really are, not just their success.

When letter c) is your most frequent selection, you're probably a ZEBRA.

These unique, fun-loving creatures delight in being quirky innovators and creative catalysts. While their stripes may be black and white, zebras revel in shades of gray, comfortable with tension, compromise, and collaboration. They like original ideas and value taking risks to explore new possibilities. Often attracted to other zebras, they nonetheless enjoy mingling with the diverse menagerie of personality types they encounter.

GIRAFFES rise above your other options if you most often chose d).

A natural motivator who doesn't mind standing out in the crowd, giraffes keep their eyes on what's ahead and usually lead from the top down. They command respect for their natural abilities and unself-conscious ability to remain focused on the big picture. Giraffes never apologize

124

for delegating the details to others below them. While traditional in many ways, these visionaries create lasting legacies by assembling a diverse team around shared goals.

If you chose e) more than other responses, then you might be a CHEETAH.

Fast, fierce, and fun-loving, cheetahs are clever communicators who often blend in to their surroundings until it's time to attack a problem. Then they stand out with their speed, efficiency, and social acumen. Rarely alone, they often travel with a tight group of friends, chasing the latest trends and creating some of their own. Cheetahs have a great sense of style and are often charming, entertaining, and spontaneous.

If letter f) expresses your responses most often, then you're likely a GAZELLE.

These graceful, quick-thinking, highly responsive types rarely stand still and are natural multi-taskers. Gazelles use their speed to accomplish goals but may need to slow down to allow others to catch up and appreciate their trailblazing work. With an athletic intensity, these sleek masters of efficiency react well in a crisis, taking necessary actions immediately. Gazelles stay busy and tend to be incredibly productive in almost all areas.

NOTES

NOTES

NOTES